I have great hope for this upcoming generation of students. I believe they are hungry for God. And I'm thankful for resources like Andy Klenke's *Experience the Wisdom of Proverbs* that will equip these teens to engage with Scripture in meaningful ways. Klenke does a great job drawing out the wisdom embedded in Solomon's collection of proverbs and leads students through a variety of exercises to apply that wisdom directly to their lives. Students will find this resource understandable, relatable, and practical.

Tammy Melchien, teaching team pastor at Community Christian Church

Experience the Wisdom of Proverbs invites students to gain wisdom by going right to the Scriptures. The hands-on assignments welcome reflection without bogging [students] down in the details, a perennial problem for anyone who sits down to read through the book of Proverbs. The pace and tone of the study invite personal, thoughtful application. Solomon himself couldn't have asked for more.

Norman Hubbard, author and collegiate ministry staff member with The Navigators

When my boys were small, I adopted a nightly prayer over them: *Dear God, give my sons wisdom to know right from wrong, and give them the courage to do right—even when it's hard.* Now that they are young men, I rejoice to see God answering this prayer in mighty ways—including with this resource. *Experience the Wisdom of Proverbs* is a powerful guide to a Powerful Guide, written in a language we can all understand.

Tricia Lott Williford, author of *This Book Is for You* and coauthor of *You Are Safe Now*

EXPERIENCE
THE WISDOM OF
proverbs

31 Days of Reading, Learning, and Living God's Word

Andy Klenke

A NavPress resource published in alliance
with Tyndale House Publishers

NavPress.com

Experience the Wisdom of Proverbs: 31 Days of Reading, Learning, and Living God's Word

Copyright © 2024 by Experience Scripture. All rights reserved.

A NavPress resource published in alliance with Tyndale House Publishers

Adapted from *Experience the Wisdom of Proverbs* copyright © 2022 by Experience Scripture, xpscripture.com

NavPress, the NavPress logo, *The Message*, and *The Message* logo are registered trademarks of NavPress, The Navigators, Colorado Springs, CO. *Tyndale* is a registered trademark of Tyndale House Ministries. Absence of ® in connection with marks of NavPress or other parties does not indicate an absence of registration of those marks.

The Team:
David Zimmerman, Publisher; Olivia Eldredge, Managing Editor; Jennifer L. Phelps, Designer; Sarah K. Johnson, Proofreading Coordinator

Cover and interior illustration of dot pattern copyright © K J Pargeter/Freepik.com. All rights reserved. Cover and interior illustration of circle created by Jennifer L. Phelps. Copyright © 2024 by Tyndale House Ministries. All rights reserved.

Interior illustration of compass rose copyright © by NAPISAH/thenounproject.com. All rights reserved.

Author photo copyright © 2023 by Tim Tab Studios. All rights reserved.

The Message: The Bible in Contemporary Language copyright © 1993, 2002, 2018 by Eugene H. Peterson. All rights reserved. *The Message: The Bible in Contemporary Language* Numbered Edition copyright © 2005.

Some of the anecdotal illustrations in this book are true to life and are included with the permission of the persons involved. All other illustrations are composites of real situations, and any resemblance to people living or dead is purely coincidental.

For information about special discounts for bulk purchases, please contact Tyndale House Publishers at csresponse@tyndale.com, or call 1-855-277-9400.

ISBN 978-1-64158-915-4

Printed in China

30	29	28	27	26	25	24
7	6	5	4	3	2	1

contents

introduction

Did you know that you can use Proverbs almost every day?

You make hundreds of decisions every day. Some big, some small. You choose what you wear, what you eat, who you talk to, what you say, how you spend your time, money, and energy. You choose whether or not you will stay up late to finish a season of your favorite show. You choose whether you are going to introduce yourself to the new kid in school who has no one to sit with at lunch. You choose whether you will listen to your parents the first time they ask you to do your chores or finish your homework. You choose how long you spend scrolling and posting on social media. Your life is made up of thousands upon thousands of choices. The question is, are you choosing wisely?

This is where Proverbs comes in. Proverbs is a book of wise advice and is meant to be used as a helpful tool to navigate daily decisions. And while some decisions may not seem like a big deal right now, our decisions now impact the habits and values we form as we get older. As you will quickly learn as you read this book, Proverbs contains wisdom for day-to-day life that is just as applicable to you in the twenty-first century as it was when it was written.

King Solomon, the author of most of the Proverbs, had a son named Rehoboam. As a way to prepare his son for the realities of this world, Solomon wrote down his advice in the book we now call Proverbs.

Author. Mostly Solomon

Purpose. To equip those who follow God to live a wise, God-honoring life.

Style. Quick, two-line statements about the realities of life. (These little phrases are also called *aphorisms*.)

Key verses.

> Trust GOD from the bottom of your heart;
>> don't try to figure out everything on your own.
> Listen for GOD's voice in everything you do, everywhere you go;
>> he's the one who will keep you on track.
>
> PROVERBS 3:5-6

Themes.

- *Wisdom*: Proverbs is very concerned with helping people make wise decisions that honor God and lead to a flourishing life!
- *Foolishness*: Proverbs has harsh words for those who do not prioritize wisdom and instead choose a life of foolishness.
- *Wealth*: Proverbs has much to say about the role that money and wealth play in our ability to live a God-honoring life.
- *Caring for those in need*: Throughout the book, Proverbs highlights that wise people will care for those in need.

Major characters.

- *Solomon*: King David's son and the primary author of Proverbs. In addition to being one of the wealthiest people to ever live, Solomon is also considered to be one of the wisest people in history.
- *Lady Wisdom*: Lady Wisdom is a fictional character Solomon uses to help us understand what wisdom truly looks like.
- *Madame Prostitute*: Madame Prostitute (sometimes called Lady Folly) is a fictional character who represents foolishness and unwise behavior.

how to get the most out of this book

This book, divided into thirty-one days of reading, learning, and living, is designed to help you experience Scripture. Use these step-by-step instructions to help understand how you can best use this tool.

Know before You Go

This section explains the background information you need in order to understand the day's Scripture. In other words, it gives some ideas for you to know before you go and read.

Read the Passage

The Scripture for the day's experience will be printed using *The Message* version of the Bible. Do not skip this reading! This is the most important step in your experience.

After the Passage

This section explores the messages, themes, or confusing parts in the day's Scripture. It is not meant to be the answer key, since we will not address every question or issue that you may have after reading the passage. The point is to introduce you to Scripture and help you understand the main idea, or bottom line, for each day.

The Bottom Line

This short statement distills the passage into a core concept for you to continue to reflect on.

Experience

This section creates space for you to process or experience each day's Scripture. The questions are meant to engage different parts of your mind, so each day's experience will vary in style. We want you to go beyond simply reading Proverbs. We want you to experience its truth for yourself. Take time to respond to the questions provided and be honest with yourself as you experience Scripture. Do not feel boxed in by the questions! Use this space to explore what God is teaching you.

Takeaway and Pray

This section prompts you to choose one personal application. Consider the ideas you have processed and commit to one as your main takeaway. Then focus your daily prayer on one specific request, confession, and/or praise. Naming this one specific prayer allows you to reflect on God's power and possible answer to prayer as time passes.

WE ARE EXCITED FOR
YOU TO EXPERIENCE THE
WISDOM OF PROVERBS
OVER THE NEXT
THIRTY-ONE DAYS!

wisdom for all

Proverbs 1

Know before You Go

King Solomon shares the importance of wisdom and how it benefits us at every stage of life.

Read the Passage

1:1-6 These are the wise sayings of Solomon,
    David's son, Israel's king—
Written down so we'll know how to live well and right,
    to understand what life means and where it's going;
A manual for living,
    for learning what's right and just and fair;
To teach the inexperienced the ropes
    and give our young people a grasp on reality.
There's something here also for seasoned men and women,
    still a thing or two for the experienced to learn—
Fresh wisdom to probe and penetrate,
    the rhymes and reasons of wise men and women.

[7] Start with God—the first step in learning is bowing down to God;
  only fools thumb their noses at such wisdom and learning.

[8-19] Pay close attention, friend, to what your father tells you;
    never forget what you learned at your mother's knee.
  Wear their counsel like a winning crown,
    like rings on your fingers.
  Dear friend, if bad companions tempt you,
    don't go along with them.
  If they say—"Let's go out and raise some hell.
    Let's beat up some old man, mug some old woman.
  Let's pick them clean
    and get them ready for their funerals.
  We'll load up on top-quality loot.
    We'll haul it home by the truckload.
  Join us for the time of your life!
    With us, it's share and share alike!"—
  Oh, friend, don't give them a second look;
    don't listen to them for a minute.
  They're racing to a very bad end,
    hurrying to ruin everything they lay hands on.
  Nobody robs a bank
    with everyone watching,
  Yet that's what these people are doing—
    they're doing themselves in.
  When you grab all you can get, that's what happens:
    the more you get, the less you are.
[20-21] Lady Wisdom goes out in the street and shouts.
    At the town center she makes her speech.
  In the middle of the traffic she takes her stand.
    At the busiest corner she calls out:

22-24 "Simpletons! How long will you wallow in ignorance?
  Cynics! How long will you feed your cynicism?
Idiots! How long will you refuse to learn?
  About face! I can revise your life.
Look, I'm ready to pour out my spirit on you;
  I'm ready to tell you all I know.
As it is, I've called, but you've turned a deaf ear;
  I've reached out to you, but you've ignored me.

25-28 "Since you laugh at my counsel
  and make a joke of my advice,
How can I take you seriously?
  I'll turn the tables and joke about *your* troubles!
What if the roof falls in,
  and your whole life goes to pieces?
What if catastrophe strikes and there's nothing
  to show for your life but rubble and ashes?
You'll need me then. You'll call for me, but don't expect
  an answer.
  No matter how hard you look, you won't find me.

29-33 "Because you hated Knowledge
  and had nothing to do with the Fear-of-God,
Because you wouldn't take my advice
  and brushed aside all my offers to train you,
Well, you've made your bed—now lie in it;
  you wanted your own way—now, how do you like it?
Don't you see what happens, you simpletons, you idiots?
  Carelessness kills; complacency is murder.
First pay attention to me, and then relax.
  Now you can take it easy—you're in good hands."

After the Passage

In his prologue, King Solomon gets right to the point in sharing why reading Proverbs is so important. With each new line, Solomon introduces a new reason why reading Proverbs is essential.

While Solomon wrote specifically to a "friend" (his son, Rehoboam), he describes several types of people who would also benefit from reading Proverbs. Reread Proverbs 1:1-7 to review the people and purposes Solomon mentions.

(*Hint:* If Solomon doesn't mention a specific type of person, it's meant for everyone.)

FOR	WHY PROVERBS IS IMPORTANT	WHOM IT BENEFITS
#1		
#2		
#3		
#4		

Solomon covers a wide range of people who will benefit from Proverbs, but he also points out one type of person who will never find Proverbs helpful: *the fool.*

The Bottom Line

The advice in Proverbs is helpful for every person in every stage of life.

EXPERIENCE

Who are the two wisest people you know? Ask them the following questions.

QUESTIONS	PERSON 1	PERSON 2
How did you gain wisdom?		
What is one piece of advice you have for me?		

Takeaway and Pray

My takeaway from this experience is

My prayer today is a

__ REQUEST   __ CONFESSION   __ PRAISE

a worthy quest

Proverbs 2

Know before You Go

Solomon compares wisdom to hidden treasure and explains how it protects us from wickedness.

Read the Passage

2:1-5 Good friend, take to heart what I'm telling you;
     collect my counsels and guard them with your life.
Tune your ears to the world of Wisdom;
     set your heart on a life of Understanding.
That's right—if you make Insight your priority,
     and won't take no for an answer,
Searching for it like a prospector panning for gold,
     like an adventurer on a treasure hunt,
Believe me, before you know it Fear-of-God will be yours;
     you'll have come upon the Knowledge of God.

6-8 And here's why: GOD gives out Wisdom free,
    is plainspoken in Knowledge and Understanding.
He's a rich mine of Common Sense for those who live well,
    a personal bodyguard to the candid and sincere.
He keeps his eye on all who live honestly,
    and pays special attention to his loyally committed ones.

9-15 So now you can pick out what's true and fair,
    find all the good trails!
Lady Wisdom will be your close friend,
    and Brother Knowledge your pleasant companion.
Good Sense will scout ahead for danger,
    Insight will keep an eye out for you.
They'll keep you from making wrong turns,
    or following the bad directions
Of those who are lost themselves
    and can't tell a trail from a tumbleweed,
These losers who make a game of evil
    and throw parties to celebrate perversity,
Traveling paths that go nowhere,
    wandering in a maze of detours and dead ends.

16-19 Wise friends will rescue you from the Temptress—
    that smooth-talking Seductress
Who's faithless to the husband she married years ago,
    never gave a second thought to her promises before God.
Her whole way of life is doomed;
    every step she takes brings her closer to hell.
No one who joins her company ever comes back,
    ever sets foot on the path to real living.

²⁰⁻²² So—join the company of good men and women,
  keep your feet on the tried-and-true paths.
It's the men who walk straight who will settle this land,
  the women with integrity who will last here.
The corrupt will lose their lives;
  the dishonest will be gone for good.

After the Passage

While Proverbs 1 helps us understand the meaning of wisdom, Proverbs 2 helps us understand how to find wisdom. Thousands of years before movies and cartoons, people dreamt about finding hidden treasure—so much so that Solomon uses this image in Proverbs 2:1-5 to describe the way we should search for wisdom.

Before you say, "I'm too old to believe in searching for hidden treasure," consider what would happen if you received a legitimate, credible tip that buried somewhere in your neighborhood was a chest full of money. You would likely get up early and stay up late looking for it. You would probably spend your free time researching probable locations and tracking down clues. There is no way you would give up if a few of your ideas did not pan out or if you did not find it after just a few days. Why? Because a chest full of money could change your life! This kind of quest, with all the excitement and hard work, is the image Solomon is using to illustrate how we should search for wisdom.

The treasure hunt image conveys two sides of the same coin. It conveys both the way we should search for wisdom and the tremendous value of wisdom—more valuable than silver or hidden treasure! In fact, Proverbs 2:9-19 explains that the value of wisdom is its ability to protect us from all kinds of wickedness and poor decisions (described as "the Temptress" or "Seductress").

Meanwhile, in Proverbs 2:6-8, Solomon reminds us that we are not on this quest by ourselves. While we search for wisdom, God is

- giving out wisdom freely,
- guarding us,

- keeping an eye on us, and
- paying special attention to us.

The Bottom Line

We should search for wisdom as if it were a hidden treasure (and we have the map!).

EXPERIENCE

On a scale from 1 to 10 (1 being *not at all* and 10 being *absolutely*), how do these factors hinder your quest for wisdom?

	1	2	3	4	5	6	7	8	9	10
busyness	1	2	3	4	5	6	7	8	9	10
laziness	1	2	3	4	5	6	7	8	9	10
peer pressure	1	2	3	4	5	6	7	8	9	10
uncertainty	1	2	3	4	5	6	7	8	9	10
stubbornness	1	2	3	4	5	6	7	8	9	10
lack of prioritizing	1	2	3	4	5	6	7	8	9	10

Pick the factor with the highest score. What is one way you can minimize its impact on your quest for wisdom this week?

 Draw a compass somewhere you will see it frequently (on a notebook or on a sticky note for your car or locker or room). Let the compass remind you that you are on a quest for wisdom!

Takeaway and Pray

My takeaway from this experience is

My prayer today is a

__ REQUEST __ CONFESSION __ PRAISE

the lighthouse

Proverbs 3

Know before You Go

Solomon explains the importance of trusting God's wisdom rather than our own.

Read the Passage

¹⁻² Good friend, don't forget all I've taught you;
    take to heart my commands.
They'll help you live a long, long time,
    a long life lived full and well.

³⁻⁴ Don't lose your grip on Love and Loyalty.
    Tie them around your neck; carve their initials on your heart.
Earn a reputation for living well
    in God's eyes and the eyes of the people.

⁵⁻¹² Trust GOD from the bottom of your heart;
    don't try to figure out everything on your own.

Listen for GOD's voice in everything you do, everywhere you go;
    he's the one who will keep you on track.
Don't assume that you know it all.
    Run to GOD! Run from evil!
Your body will glow with health,
    your very bones will vibrate with life!
Honor GOD with everything you own;
    give him the first and the best.
Your barns will burst,
    your wine vats will brim over.
But don't, dear friend, resent GOD's discipline;
    don't sulk under his loving correction.
It's the child he loves that GOD corrects;
    a father's delight is behind all this.

13-18 You're blessed when you meet Lady Wisdom,
    when you make friends with Madame Insight.
She's worth far more than money in the bank;
    her friendship is better than a big salary.
Her value exceeds all the trappings of wealth;
    nothing you could wish for holds a candle to her.
With one hand she gives long life,
    with the other she confers recognition.
Her manner is beautiful,
    her life wonderfully complete.
She's the very Tree of Life to those who embrace her.
    Hold her tight—and be blessed!

19-20 With Lady Wisdom, GOD formed Earth;
    with Madame Insight, he raised Heaven.
They knew when to signal rivers and springs to the surface,
    and dew to descend from the night skies.

21-26 Dear friend, guard Clear Thinking and Common Sense
  with your life;
 don't for a minute lose sight of them.
They'll keep your soul alive and well,
 they'll keep you fit and attractive.
You'll travel safely,
 you'll neither tire nor trip.
You'll take afternoon naps without a worry,
 you'll enjoy a good night's sleep.
No need to panic over alarms or surprises,
 or predictions that doomsday's just around the corner,
Because GOD will be right there with you;
 he'll keep you safe and sound.

27-29 Never walk away from someone who deserves help;
 your hand is *God's* hand for that person.
Don't tell your neighbor "Maybe some other time"
 or "Try me tomorrow"
 when the money's right there in your pocket.
Don't figure ways of taking advantage of your neighbor
 when he's sitting there trusting and unsuspecting.

30-32 Don't walk around with a chip on your shoulder,
 always spoiling for a fight.
Don't try to be like those who shoulder their way through life.
 Why be a bully?
"Why not?" you say. Because GOD can't stand twisted souls.
 It's the straightforward who get his respect.

33-35 GOD's curse blights the house of the wicked,
 but he blesses the home of the righteous.

He gives proud skeptics a cold shoulder,
>   but if you're down on your luck, he's right there to help.
Wise living gets rewarded with honor;
>   stupid living gets the booby prize.

After the Passage

Proverbs 3:5-6 is one of the most well-known passages in the Bible. These two verses could be the theme of the entire book of Proverbs, since they acknowledge our tendency to trust our own wisdom yet urge us to trust in God's ways instead.

> Trust GOD from the bottom of your heart;
>   don't try to figure out everything on your own.
> Listen for GOD's voice in everything you do, everywhere you go;
>   he's the one who will keep you on track.
> PROVERBS 3:5-6

Only God, in His infinite wisdom, knows all the answers that will lead to the full and abundant life He desires for us. Since this is the case, we should seek Him daily to ask Him to help us make good decisions and lead us on the right path.

Imagine you are walking on a sandy beach. Off in the distance, you see an incredible lighthouse that you decide you want to explore. From far away, the sand leading to the lighthouse looks smooth and clear, so you start to sprint in its direction. But, as you get closer, you start to feel pain on the bottom of your feet. Looking down, you notice you have been running along sharp rocks that have washed onto the shore that you originally did not see. You have no choice but to slow down and carefully place each step to avoid more sharp rocks. Some of your steps seem like they are a bit out of the way, but you are avoiding the dangerous path. While your new pace is slow and takes a lot of patience, you finally reach the lighthouse safely. As you look behind you, you see that your trail of footprints is actually stretched out in a straight line!

This is the message of Proverbs 3. We should carefully look at every step in our life to avoid making decisions that are not healthy or God-honoring. Sometimes the path right in front of us looks like a sandy beach when it is actually covered with rocks just beneath the surface. Sometimes the path that looks like it is a detour is actually the straightest and safest path to take. Our job is to simply focus on each step we take and trust that God is making our paths straight.

The Bottom Line

Trusting in God's wisdom is always better than trusting in our own wisdom.

EXPERIENCE

Memorize Proverbs 3:5-6. Having these verses in your head can help motivate you to make wise decisions and remind you to trust God's path.

Memorizing Scripture can be difficult! Here are a few tips that may help:

- Start small. Proverbs 3:5-6 is four lines of text.
- Write out the verses multiple times. Studies show that writing by hand increases our ability to remember things.
- Read the verses out loud and on repeat. This process will help cement the verses in your head.
- Ask someone to memorize these verses with you. Having the extra help and accountability can be a big encouragement!
- Try memorizing the passage one line at a time rather than trying to memorize the whole thing at once.

Here's the passage again:

> Trust GOD from the bottom of your heart;
>   don't try to figure out everything on your own.
> Listen for GOD's voice in everything you do, everywhere you go;
>   he's the one who will keep you on track.
> PROVERBS 3:5-6

Takeaway and Pray

My takeaway from this experience is

My prayer today is a

__ REQUEST __ CONFESSION __ PRAISE

wisdom as a woman

Proverbs 4

Know before You Go

Solomon introduces wisdom as a woman and explains the rewards of listening to her.

Read the Passage

¹⁻² Listen, friends, to some fatherly advice;
    sit up and take notice so you'll know how to live.
I'm giving you good counsel;
    don't let it go in one ear and out the other.

³⁻⁹ When I was a boy at my father's knee,
    the pride and joy of my mother,
He would sit me down and drill me:
    "Take this to heart. Do what I tell you—live!
Sell everything and buy Wisdom! Forage for Understanding!
    Don't forget one word! Don't deviate an inch!
Never walk away from Wisdom—she guards your life;
    love her—she keeps her eye on you.

Above all and before all, do this: Get Wisdom!
    Write this at the top of your list: Get Understanding!
Throw your arms around her—believe me, you won't regret it;
    never let her go—she'll make your life glorious.
She'll garland your life with grace,
    she'll festoon your days with beauty."

10-15 Dear friend, take my advice;
    it will add years to your life.
I'm writing out clear directions to Wisdom Way,
    I'm drawing a map to Righteous Road.
I don't want you ending up in blind alleys,
    or wasting time making wrong turns.
Hold tight to good advice; don't relax your grip.
    Guard it well—your life is at stake!
Don't take Wicked Bypass;
    don't so much as set foot on that road.
Stay clear of it; give it a wide berth.
    Make a detour and be on your way.

16-17 Evil people are restless
    unless they're making trouble;
They can't get a good night's sleep
    unless they've made life miserable for somebody.
Perversity is their food and drink,
    violence their drug of choice.

18-19 The ways of right-living people glow with light;
    the longer they live, the brighter they shine.
But the road of wrongdoing gets darker and darker—
    travelers can't see a thing; they fall flat on their faces.

20-22 Dear friend, listen well to my words;
>   tune your ears to my voice.
> Keep my message in plain view at all times.
>   Concentrate! Learn it by heart!
> Those who discover these words live, really live;
>   body and soul, they're bursting with health.

23-27 Keep vigilant watch over your heart;
>   *that's* where life starts.
> Don't talk out of both sides of your mouth;
>   avoid careless banter, white lies, and gossip.
> Keep your eyes straight ahead;
>   ignore all sideshow distractions.
> Watch your step,
>   and the road will stretch out smooth before you.
> Look neither right nor left;
>   leave evil in the dust.

After the Passage

Maybe you've noticed that Solomon loves to use all sorts of writing tricks to make his messages about wisdom more interesting. Here in Proverbs 4, Solomon personifies wisdom, giving it human characteristics to help deepen our understanding and appreciation of its rewards.

While there may be a lot of interesting reasons Solomon describes wisdom as a woman, one reason is certainly because, similar to Spanish (*la guitarra* for *the guitar*), French (*le chien* for *the dog*), and other languages, Hebrew (the original language of the book of Proverbs) associates each word with a particular gender, and the word Solomon uses for *wisdom* here is a feminine word.

Solomon offers instructions about the pursuit of wisdom, but he also points to the rewards of wisdom, as we see in Proverbs 4:3-12.

COMMANDS FOR WISDOM	REWARDS OF WISDOM
Sell everything and buy wisdom.	
	She guards your life.
Forage for understanding.	
	She keeps her eye on you.
Never walk away from her.	
	She'll make your life glorious.
Love her.	
	She'll garland your life with grace.
Throw your arms around her.	
	She'll festoon your days with beauty.
Never let her go.	

The Bottom Line

Wisdom will always reward you.

EXPERIENCE

Wisdom will always reward you, but recognizing wisdom's rewards can be a challenge. When we think of rewards, we tend to think of things like money, medals, certificates, or prizes. But wisdom's rewards may be more subtle—and actually more valuable! The rewards of wisdom may include a clear conscience, more time in your day, deeper relationships—the list could go on and on! Take some time to think about potential rewards for the following wise choices.

WISE CHOICE	POTENTIAL REWARD
saving your money	
finishing your homework	
going to bed at a sensible time	
obeying your parents	
eating healthy	
avoiding temptation	
choosing good friends	

Takeaway and Pray

My takeaway from this experience is

My prayer today is a

__ REQUEST   __ CONFESSION   __ PRAISE

temptation as a woman too?

Proverbs 5

Know before You Go

Proverbs 5 introduces us to a woman very different from Wisdom.

Read the Passage

1-2 Dear friend, pay close attention to this, my wisdom;
    listen very closely to the way I see it.
Then you'll acquire a taste for good sense;
    what I tell you will keep you out of trouble.

3-6 The lips of a seductive woman are oh so sweet,
    her soft words are oh so smooth.
But it won't be long before she's gravel in your mouth,
    a pain in your gut, a wound in your heart.

She's dancing down the perfumed path to Death;
     she's headed straight for Hell and taking you with her.
She hasn't a clue about Real Life,
     about who she is or where she's going.

7-14 So, my friend, listen closely;
     don't treat my words casually.
Keep your distance from such a woman;
     absolutely stay out of her neighborhood.
You don't want to squander your wonderful life,
     to waste your precious life among the hardhearted.
Why should you allow strangers to take advantage of you?
     Why be exploited by those who care nothing for you?
You don't want to end your life full of regrets,
     nothing but sin and bones,
Saying, "Oh, why didn't I do what they told me?
     Why did I reject a disciplined life?
Why didn't I listen to my mentors,
     or take my teachers seriously?
My life is ruined!
     I haven't one blessed thing to show for my life!"

15-16 Do you know the saying, "Drink from your own rain barrel,
     draw water from your own spring-fed well"?
It's true. Otherwise, you may one day come home
     and find your barrel empty and your well polluted.

17-20 Your spring water is for you and you only,
     not to be passed around among strangers.

Bless your fresh-flowing fountain!
    Enjoy the wife you married as a young man!
Lovely as an angel, beautiful as a rose—
    don't ever quit taking delight in her body.
    Never take her love for granted!
Why would you trade enduring intimacies for cheap thrills with a prostitute?
    for dalliance with a promiscuous stranger?

[21-23] Mark well that GOD doesn't miss a move you make;
    he's aware of every step you take.
The shadow of your sin will overtake you;
    you'll find yourself stumbling all over yourself in the dark.
Death is the reward of an undisciplined life;
    your foolish decisions trap you in a dead end.

After the Passage

We should not be surprised, having met the woman Wisdom in Proverbs 4, to see another woman enter the scene. The opposite of wisdom—temptation of all kinds—is personified in Proverbs 5 as a seductive woman. Having commanded us to search after wisdom in chapter 4, here Solomon tells us to stay as far away from temptation as possible. "Absolutely stay out of her neighborhood," he tells us in Proverbs 5:8. (Throughout this study, I'll refer to this recurring character as "Temptation.")

As we'll see in later chapters, Temptation is a master at coaxing people into sin. Every kind of temptation does this to us in its own way. We think we are wise enough to make good decisions without seeking God's wisdom, but Solomon encourages us to look beyond the appeal of temptation to the crooked, dark, messy paths it leads us on.

The following chart contrasts Wisdom and Temptation in Proverbs 4 and 5.

WISDOM	TEMPTATION
Searching after Wisdom is hard work.	Temptation seems appealing and unthreatening.
Wisdom has inherent benefits.	Before long, Temptation is "gravel in your mouth" (Proverbs 5:4).
We are protected by Wisdom.	Temptation "hasn't a clue about Real Life" (Proverbs 5:6).
Wisdom belongs "at the top of your list" (Proverbs 4:7).	Temptation ultimately harms your heart.
Wisdom will "add years to your life" (Proverbs 4:10).	Temptation will lead you down crooked paths to death.

The Bottom Line

Temptation tells one lie after another.

EXPERIENCE

Given how Proverbs 5 is written, we might think it's specifically about sexual tempta-tion. But while sexual temptation is most definitely dangerous and should be avoided, every type of temptation we face in life lies to us and leads us to believe its way is better than God's way. Ultimately, giving in to temptation leads to disappointment.

It is important to remember that Solomon is not telling us that being tempted is a sin. Even Jesus was tempted! The wisest path for us, however, is the path that avoids temptation altogether. (We'll come back to this idea when we read Proverbs 7.)

What is one of your biggest temptations?

Write out a prayer asking God to help you resist this temptation. Read this prayer every morning for the next week.

Takeaway and Pray

My takeaway from this experience is

My prayer today is a

__ REQUEST __ CONFESSION __ PRAISE

small but wise

Proverbs 6

Know before You Go

Solomon uses an ant to illustrate a wise work ethic.

Read the Passage

¹⁻⁵ Dear friend, if you've gone into hock with your neighbor
    or locked yourself into a deal with a stranger,
If you've impulsively promised the shirt off your back
    and now find yourself shivering out in the cold,
Friend, don't waste a minute, get yourself out of that mess.
    You're in that man's clutches!
    Go, put on a long face; act desperate.
Don't procrastinate—
    there's no time to lose.
Run like a deer from the hunter,
    fly like a bird from the trapper!

⁶⁻¹¹ You lazy fool, look at an ant.
>   Watch it closely; let it teach you a thing or two.
> Nobody has to tell it what to do.
>   All summer it stores up food;
>   at harvest it stockpiles provisions.
> So how long are you going to laze around doing nothing?
>   How long before you get out of bed?
> A nap here, a nap there, a day off here, a day off there,
>   sit back, take it easy—do you know what comes next?
> Just this: You can look forward to a dirt-poor life,
>   poverty your permanent houseguest!

¹²⁻¹⁵ Swindlers and scoundrels
>   talk out of both sides of their mouths.
> They wink at each other, they shuffle their feet,
>   they cross their fingers behind their backs.
> Their perverse minds are always cooking up something nasty,
>   always stirring up trouble.
> Catastrophe is just around the corner for them,
>   a total wreck, their lives ruined beyond repair.

¹⁶⁻¹⁹ Here are six things GOD hates,
>   and one more that he loathes with a passion:

>   eyes that are arrogant,
>   a tongue that lies,
>   hands that murder the innocent,
>   a heart that hatches evil plots,
>   feet that race down a wicked track,
>   a mouth that lies under oath,
>   a troublemaker in the family.

20-23 Good friend, follow your father's good advice;
  don't wander off from your mother's teachings.
Wrap yourself in them from head to foot;
  wear them like a scarf around your neck.
Wherever you walk, they'll guide you;
  whenever you rest, they'll guard you;
  when you wake up, they'll tell you what's next.
For sound advice is a beacon,
  good teaching is a light,
  moral discipline is a life path.

24-35 They'll protect you from promiscuous women,
  from the seductive talk of some temptress.
Don't lustfully fantasize on her beauty,
  nor be taken in by her bedroom eyes.
You can buy an hour with a prostitute for a loaf of bread,
  but a promiscuous woman may well eat *you* alive.
Can you build a fire in your lap
  and not burn your pants?
Can you walk barefoot on hot coals
  and not get blisters?
It's the same when you have sex with your neighbor's wife:
  Touch her and you'll pay for it. No excuses.
Hunger is no excuse
  for a thief to steal;
When he's caught he has to pay it back,
  even if he has to put his whole house in hock.
Adultery is a brainless act,
  soul-destroying, self-destructive;
Expect a bloody nose, a black eye,
  and a reputation ruined for good.

For jealousy detonates rage in a cheated husband;
wild for revenge, he won't make allowances.
Nothing you say or pay will make it all right;
neither bribes nor reason will satisfy him.

After the Passage

Proverbs 6 is a great example of how practical the book of Proverbs is for our everyday life. The advice given by Solomon is very simple (though not easy). By using an ant as an example, Solomon encourages us to work hard and avoid laziness.

Of all the beautiful animals on Earth, why should we imitate the ant? First and foremost, Solomon draws our attention to the ant's undeniable work ethic. You rarely see an ant that is not moving feverishly. They are constantly working. Solomon also mentions that ants do not need anyone to tell them to work—they are self-starters. Last, ants prepare for the future. They store food in anticipation of the winter and are ready for hard times. All these characteristics are praiseworthy and are part of living a wise life.

The chapter goes on to describe the opposite work ethic. Sluggards sleep off their worries and responsibilities rather than facing them. While the ant is ready for whatever comes, the sluggard is completely unprepared when problems show up. The sluggard's life is marked by slowness, laziness, and irresponsibility. Solomon uses these two images from everyday life to remind us that working hard is always a wiser decision than being lazy.

The Bottom Line

Working hard is always wiser than being lazy.

EXPERIENCE

Be honest with yourself: Are you more of a sluggard or an ant? Where would you place yourself on this line?

SLUGGARD   **ANT**

What is one area in your life where you could be more like an ant? Your job? Your schoolwork? Your health? Your chores? Something you want to accomplish? Something else?

What is one way you can be more of an ant than a sluggard this week?

FROM NOW ON, WHEN YOU SEE AN ANT, REMEMBER PROVERBS 6!

One reason Solomon and other biblical authors use everyday images like ants (or trees or stars or grass) is that we interact with and observe these images so often. Almost everyone is familiar with how ants work, or how a tree grows, or how stars shine. Such images can become constant reminders of God's truth and instructions for us. From now on, when you see an ant, remember Proverbs 6!

Takeaway and Pray

My takeaway from this experience is

My prayer today is a

___ REQUEST ___ CONFESSION ___ PRAISE

red flags everywhere

Proverbs 7

Know before You Go

Solomon tells us a story about a foolish young man who meets Temptation from Proverbs 5.

Read the Passage

1-5 Dear friend, do what I tell you;
  treasure my careful instructions.
Do what I say and you'll live well.
  My teaching is as precious as your eyesight—guard it!
Write it out on the back of your hands;
  etch it on the chambers of your heart.
Talk to Wisdom as to a sister.
  Treat Insight as your companion.
They'll be with you to fend off the Temptress—
  that smooth-talking, honey-tongued Seductress.

6-12 As I stood at the window of my house
      looking out through the shutters,
Watching the mindless crowd stroll by,
      I spotted a young man without any sense
Arriving at the corner of the street where she lived,
      then turning up the path to her house.
It was dusk, the evening coming on,
      the darkness thickening into night.
Just then, a woman met him—
      she'd been lying in wait for him, dressed to seduce him.
Brazen and brash she was,
      restless and roaming, never at home,
Walking the streets, loitering in the mall,
      hanging out at every corner in town.

13-20 She threw her arms around him and kissed him,
      boldly took his arm and said,
"I've got all the makings for a feast—
      today I made my offerings, my vows are all paid,
So now I've come to find you,
      hoping to catch sight of your face—and here you are!
I've spread fresh, clean sheets on my bed,
      colorful imported linens.
My bed is aromatic with spices
      and exotic fragrances.
Come, let's make love all night,
      spend the night in ecstatic lovemaking!
My husband's not home; he's away on business,
      and he won't be back for a month."

21-23 Soon she has him eating out of her hand,
     bewitched by her honeyed speech.
Before you know it, he's trotting behind her,
     like a calf led to the butcher shop,
Like a stag lured into ambush
     and then shot with an arrow,
Like a bird flying into a net
     not knowing that its flying life is over.

24-27 So, friends, listen to me,
     take these words of mine most seriously.
Don't fool around with a woman like that;
     don't even stroll through her neighborhood.
Countless victims come under her spell;
     she's the death of many a poor man.
She runs a halfway house to hell,
     fits you out with a shroud and a coffin.

After the Passage

Remember the "woman" from Proverbs 5? In Proverbs 7, Solomon once again warns us to be aware of temptation and to take steps to avoid it. Just like a preacher or teacher who tells a story to illustrate an important point, Solomon uses great storytelling to communicate the importance of avoiding temptation. In this story, Solomon describes looking down from his second-floor window and seeing a young man without any sense walking along the road. (His description of the young man as lacking sense is similar to the description of a fool or simpleton in Proverbs 1—it means he's gullible, or easily tricked.) While the parable ends with the man being destroyed (Proverbs 7:21-23), Solomon clearly points out that this man made many mistakes before the woman ever led him astray. Look at the red flags from the story:

- *Red flag #1*: The man was in the wrong part of town. He was walking on a street toward the Seductress's house, dangerously close to temptation's home turf.

- *Red flag #2*: The man was out at the wrong time. You may have heard the phrase *Nothing good happens after midnight*. Whether in movies, literature, poetry, or music, night is typically used to describe a secretive situation. Nighttime is a clue that he was up to no good.

- *Red flag #3*: The man was in the wrong mindset. He was more interested in letting pleasure dictate his decisions than in making a wise choice.

Solomon's instruction to us through this vivid story is to avoid going down temptation's road. Even though we usually have a pretty good idea of where temptation lives, in unwise moments we choose to see just how close we can get to temptation without failing. In other words, we think we can walk down temptation's road and simply avoid temptation's house. Solomon's advice: Avoid the road altogether!

The Bottom Line

Wise decisions can minimize temptation's power.

EXPERIENCE

Look back at the temptation you wrote down on reading 5. Write it here in the box marked *Temptation*.

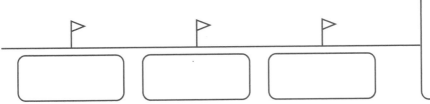

What are some red flags associated with this temptation—warnings that you may be moving toward this temptation instead of away from it? Add them to the diagram.

How can recognizing these red flags help you avoid this temptation? (For example, if your phone is a source of temptation, consider leaving it in the living room overnight—and buying an alarm clock—rather than keeping it with you. This small inconvenience can help you pursue wisdom and avoid temptation.)

Takeaway and Pray

My takeaway from this experience is

My prayer today is a

__ REQUEST __ CONFESSION __ PRAISE

wisdom in her own words

Proverbs 8

Know before You Go

Contrasting Temptation in Proverbs 7, Lady Wisdom tells her own story of success in Proverbs 8.

Read the Passage

1-11 Do you hear Lady Wisdom calling?
    Can you hear Madame Insight raising her voice?
She's taken her stand at First and Main,
    at the busiest intersection.
Right in the city square
    where the traffic is thickest, she shouts,
"You—I'm talking to all of you,
    everyone out here on the streets!
Listen, you idiots—learn good sense!
    You blockheads—shape up!
Don't miss a word of this—I'm telling you how to live well,
    I'm telling you how to live at your best.

My mouth chews and savors and relishes truth—
 I can't stand the taste of evil!
You'll only hear true and right words from my mouth;
 not one syllable will be twisted or skewed.
You'll recognize this as true—you with open minds;
 truth-ready minds will see it at once.
Prefer my life-disciplines over chasing after money,
 and God-knowledge over a lucrative career.
For Wisdom is better than all the trappings of wealth;
 nothing you could wish for holds a candle to her.

12-21 "I am Lady Wisdom, and I live next to Sanity;
 Knowledge and Discretion live just down the street.
The Fear-of-God means hating Evil,
 whose ways I hate with a passion—
 pride and arrogance and crooked talk.
Good counsel and common sense are my characteristics;
 I am both Insight and the Virtue to live it out.
With my help, leaders rule,
 and lawmakers legislate fairly;
With my help, governors govern,
 along with all in legitimate authority.
I love those who love me;
 those who look for me find me.
Wealth and Glory accompany me—
 also substantial Honor and a Good Name.
My benefits are worth more than a big salary, even a *very* big salary;
 the returns on me exceed any imaginable bonus.
You can find me on Righteous Road—that's where I walk—
 at the intersection of Justice Avenue,
Handing out life to those who love me,
 filling their arms with life—armloads of life!

²²⁻³¹ "GOD sovereignly made me—the first, the basic—
>   before he did anything else.
> I was brought into being a long time ago,
>   well before Earth got its start.
> I arrived on the scene before Ocean,
>   yes, even before Springs and Rivers and Lakes.
> Before Mountains were sculpted and Hills took shape,
>   I was already there, newborn;
> Long before GOD stretched out Earth's Horizons,
>   and tended to the minute details of Soil and Weather,
> And set Sky firmly in place,
>   I was there.
> When he mapped and gave borders to wild Ocean,
>   built the vast vault of Heaven,
>   and installed the fountains that fed Ocean,
> When he drew a boundary for Sea,
>   posted a sign that said NO TRESPASSING,
> And then staked out Earth's Foundations,
>   I was right there with him, making sure everything fit.
> Day after day I was there, with my joyful applause,
>   always enjoying his company,
> Delighted with the world of things and creatures,
>   happily celebrating the human family.

³²⁻³⁶ "So, my dear friends, listen carefully;
>   those who embrace these my ways are most blessed.
> Mark a life of discipline and live wisely;
>   don't squander your precious life.
> Blessed the man, blessed the woman, who listens to me,
>   awake and ready for me each morning,
>   alert and responsive as I start my day's work.

When you find me, you find life, real life,
to say nothing of God's good pleasure.
But if you wrong me, you damage your very soul;
when you reject me, you're flirting with death."

After the Passage

Rather than sharing another story from his own perspective, Solomon allows Wisdom to tell us a story directly. Like in Proverbs 4, this is another example of Solomon using the tool of personification.

Before Wisdom speaks, the first few verses of the chapter set the stage for her story. Here we see big differences between wisdom and temptation:

TEMPTATION (PROVERBS 7)	WISDOM (PROVERBS 8)
Temptation whispers to one person at a time.	Wisdom shouts loudly to everyone around her.
Temptation sneaks along streets at night, looking to take people by surprise.	Wisdom stands in the highest, most public place at the city gates.

Wisdom begins by grabbing the attention of everyone around her—especially the foolish. She makes a handful of incredibly bold claims: She lasts longer than any material possession, and she is more valuable than treasure. Just in case someone thinks these claims are a bit outlandish, Wisdom goes on to provide her credentials. She has been the secret tool for all great rulers and kings—including Solomon! (In 1 Kings 3:1-14, God came to Solomon and gave him the gift of wisdom, making Solomon the wisest king ever to live.)

She also explains that she's very, very old. She reminds her listeners that she has been around since the beginning of time; actually, she was there even before the beginning of time! Proverbs 8:22-31 explains that when God was designing the world, Wisdom was there watching, consulting, helping. So, while her claims may seem a bit bold, Wisdom has the credentials to back them up! Wisdom has been a part of everything that has ever been successful!

The Bottom Line

Wisdom is the main ingredient in anything that has ever been successful.

EXPERIENCE

Draw a picture of two of the most successful leaders you can think of. Around their picture, write the things these leaders did that made them so successful.

How did wisdom contribute to these leaders' actions?

Whenever you are in a situation where you need to make a decision or take action, consider how these wise leaders would respond. Picturing someone you respect acting in your situation can help you identify the wise, praiseworthy choice versus a foolish choice. Ask yourself, *Would [wise person X] do this?*

Takeaway and Pray

My takeaway from this experience is

My prayer today is a

__ REQUEST __ CONFESSION __ PRAISE

what's for dinner?

Proverbs 9

Know before You Go

Solomon describes two feasts, one hosted by Wisdom and the other hosted by Madame Prostitute.

Read the Passage

¹⁻⁶ Lady Wisdom has built and furnished her home;
  it's supported by seven hewn timbers.
The banquet meal is ready to be served: lamb roasted,
  wine poured out, table set with silver and flowers.
Having dismissed her serving maids,
  Lady Wisdom goes to town, stands in a prominent place,
  and invites everyone within sound of her voice:
"Are you confused about life, don't know what's going on?
  Come with me, oh come, have dinner with me!
I've prepared a wonderful spread—fresh-baked bread,
  roast lamb, carefully selected wines.

Leave your impoverished confusion and *live*!
    Walk up the street to a life with meaning."

―――――
―――――
―――――

7-12 If you reason with an arrogant cynic, you'll get slapped in the face;
    confront bad behavior and get a kick in the shins.
So don't waste your time on a scoffer;
    all you'll get for your pains is abuse.
But if you correct those who care about life,
    that's different—they'll love you for it!
Save your breath for the wise—they'll be wiser for it;
    tell good people what you know—they'll profit from it.
Skilled living gets its start in the Fear-of-God,
    insight into life from knowing a Holy God.
It's through me, Lady Wisdom, that your life deepens,
    and the years of your life ripen.
Live wisely and wisdom will permeate your life;
    mock life and life will mock you.

13-18 Then there's this other woman, Madame Prostitute—
    brazen, empty-headed, frivolous.
She sits on the front porch
    of her house on Main Street,
And as people walk by minding
    their own business, calls out,
"Are you confused about life, don't know what's going on?
    Steal off with me, I'll show you a good time!
    No one will ever know—I'll give you the time of your life."
But they don't know about all the skeletons in her closet,
    that all her guests end up in hell.

After the Passage

The two meals described in Proverbs 9 are yet another metaphor to highlight the differences between wisdom and foolishness. Wisdom is hard at work in her house to cook a giant feast. Even before she invites her guests, she sets the table to prepare her house for a great party. Wisdom is confident that anyone who attends will enjoy her food and wine and will leave her house better than when they arrived.

Madame Prostitute, who here represents temptation, on the other hand, is sitting on her porch (not preparing the house) and yells out to whoever passes by. There's no indication that she's prepared anything special. All she promises is a vaguely defined "good time," "the time of your life" (Proverbs 9:17). The difference between these two parties continues to illustrate the value of wisdom. Wisdom's meal is intentional and nutritious, just like wisdom. Wisdom may require a touch more effort, but it is so much better for you than foolishness. Madame Prostitute's offer is cheap, quick, and leaves you wanting more. Folly is simple and easy, but it never quite satisfies.

Between the descriptions of the two parties, Solomon slips in an incredibly insightful observation: Foolish people do not like to be corrected, but wise people are always open to learning and improving (Proverbs 9:7-12). Have you ever tried to correct someone who was being foolish? They are usually defensive, stubborn, and uninterested in your feedback, even if it is spot-on! A wise person, however, even if they are acting foolish, receives feedback as an opportunity to grow and become even more wise.

As you grow up, one of the most important qualities you can have is the willingness to receive correction. This trait sets you apart from foolish people who only continue acting foolish. Being open to feedback will make you a better student, friend, teammate, sibling, son or daughter, and leader. The wisest people in the world know that the wisest thing they can do is keep obtaining wisdom!

The Bottom Line

Wise people love feedback, while foolish people run from it.

EXPERIENCE

What is the most difficult piece of feedback you have ever received? What made it so difficult?

Think of the last time someone offered you correction or feedback. Who corrected you? What happened?

How did you respond in this situation? If you responded well, how were you able to do so?

If you did not respond well, what got in the way of a wise response?

Reflect on how the feedback you got might still help you. Then contact the person who gave you the feedback and thank them for helping you become a wiser person.

CONGRATULATIONS! YOU'VE JUST COMPLETED THE FIRST MAJOR SECTION OF THE BOOK OF PROVERBS!

Takeaway and Pray

My takeaway from this experience is

My prayer today is a

__ REQUEST __ CONFESSION __ PRAISE

let the comparisons begin!

Proverbs 10

Know before You Go

Solomon begins a new section of Proverbs that compares and contrasts wise and unwise behavior.

Read the Passage

¹ Wise son, glad father;
  stupid son, sad mother.

² Ill-gotten gain gets you nowhere;
  an honest life is immortal.

³ God won't starve an honest soul,
  but he frustrates the appetites of the wicked.

⁴ Sloth makes you poor;
  diligence brings wealth.

⁵ Make hay while the sun shines—that's smart;
  go fishing during harvest—that's stupid.

[6] Blessings accrue on a good and honest life,
   but the mouth of the wicked is a dark cave of abuse.

[7] A good and honest life is a blessed memorial;
   a wicked life leaves a rotten stench.

[8] A wise heart takes orders;
   an empty head will come unglued.

[9] Honesty lives confident and carefree,
   but Shifty is sure to be exposed.

[10] An evasive eye is a sign of trouble ahead,
   but an open, face-to-face meeting results in peace.

[11] The mouth of a good person is a deep, life-giving well,
   but the mouth of the wicked is a dark cave of abuse.

[12] Hatred starts fights,
   but love pulls a quilt over the bickering.

[13] You'll find wisdom on the lips of a person of insight,
   but the shortsighted needs a slap in the face.

[14] The wise accumulate knowledge—a true treasure;
   know-it-alls talk too much—a sheer waste.

[15] The wealth of the rich is their security;
   the poverty of the indigent is their ruin.

[16] The wage of a good person is exuberant life;
     an evil person ends up with nothing but sin.

[17] The road to life is a disciplined life;
     ignore correction and you're lost for good.

[18] Liars secretly hoard hatred;
     fools openly spread slander.

[19] The more talk, the less truth;
     the wise measure their words.

[20] The speech of a good person is worth waiting for;
     the blabber of the wicked is worthless.

[21] The talk of a good person is rich fare for many,
     but chatterboxes die of an empty heart.

[22] God's blessing makes life rich;
     nothing we do can improve on God.

[23] An empty-head thinks mischief is fun,
     but a mindful person relishes wisdom.

[24] The nightmares of the wicked come true;
     what the good people desire, they get.

[25] When the storm is over, there's nothing left of the wicked;
     good people, firm on their rock foundation, aren't even fazed.

²⁶ A lazy employee will give you nothing but trouble;
　　it's vinegar in the mouth, smoke in the eyes.

²⁷ The Fear-of-God expands your life;
　　a wicked life is a puny life.

²⁸ The aspirations of good people end in celebration;
　　the ambitions of bad people crash.

²⁹ God is solid backing to a well-lived life,
　　but he calls into question a shabby performance.

³⁰ Good people *last*—they can't be moved;
　　the wicked are here today, gone tomorrow.

³¹ A good person's mouth is a clear fountain of wisdom;
　　a foul mouth is a stagnant swamp.

³² The speech of a good person clears the air;
　　the words of the wicked pollute it.

After the Passage

Proverbs 1–9 has been an introduction to the rest of Solomon's proverbs. From here on out, Proverbs will look a little different. Solomon begins to simplify his wise advice into one- or two-sentence phrases to help us apply wisdom to our lives.

The previous chapters helped us learn the qualities of wisdom and why it is so important. In Proverbs 10, Solomon shows us what wisdom looks like on a practical level by comparing a wise son to a foolish son. You will also notice that the rest of Proverbs contains a lot of implied or explicit *but* statements used to compare and contrast wisdom and foolishness. This can be a very helpful tool because Solomon tells us not only what wisdom looks like but also what it does *not* look like. Glance through Proverbs 10 again and note some of the comparisons between a wise person and a foolish person.

"stupid son, sad mother" *but* "wise son, glad father" (Proverbs 10:1)
sloth is foolish *but* diligence is wise
hatred is foolish *but* love is wise
ignoring correction is foolish *but* discipline is wise
mischief is foolish *but* mindfulness is wise
wickedness is foolish *but* the fear of God is wise

The Bottom Line

The wise and the foolish have very little in common.

EXPERIENCE

Proverbs 10 contains a lot of comparisons between the wise person and the foolish person. Write your own two-sentence proverbs about how the wise and the foolish approach the following topics:

money

authority

relationships

forgiveness

time

purity

God

anger

Takeaway and Pray

My takeaway from this experience is

My prayer today is a

__ REQUEST __ CONFESSION __ PRAISE

people puddles

Proverbs 11

Know before You Go

Proverbs 11 shows how our actions directly influence the people around us.

Read the Passage

¹ GOD hates cheating in the marketplace;
     he loves it when business is aboveboard.

² The stuck-up fall flat on their faces,
     but down-to-earth people stand firm.

³ The integrity of the honest keeps them on track;
     the deviousness of crooks brings them to ruin.

⁴ A thick bankroll is no help when life falls apart,
     but a principled life can stand up to the worst.

[5] Moral character makes for smooth traveling;
    an evil life is a hard life.

[6] Good character is the best insurance;
    crooks get trapped in their sinful lust.

[7] When the wicked die, that's it—
    the story's over, end of hope.

[8] A good person is saved from much trouble;
    a bad person runs straight into it.

[9] The loose tongue of the godless spreads destruction;
    the common sense of the godly preserves them.

[10] When it goes well for good people, the whole town cheers;
    when it goes badly for bad people, the town celebrates.

[11] When right-living people bless the city, it flourishes;
    evil talk turns it into a ghost town in no time.

[12] Mean-spirited slander is heartless;
    quiet discretion accompanies good sense.

[13] A gadabout gossip can't be trusted with a secret,
    but someone of integrity won't violate a confidence.

[14] Without good direction, people lose their way;
    the more wise counsel you follow, the better your chances.

[15] Whoever makes deals with strangers is sure to get burned;
    if you keep a cool head, you'll avoid rash bargains.

¹⁶ A woman of gentle grace gets respect,
   but men of rough violence grab for loot.

¹⁷ When you're kind to others, you help yourself;
   when you're cruel to others, you hurt yourself.

¹⁸ Bad work gets paid with a bad check;
   good work gets solid pay.

¹⁹ Take your stand with God's loyal community and live,
   or chase after phantoms of evil and die.

²⁰ GOD can't stand deceivers,
   but oh how he relishes integrity.

²¹ Count on this: The wicked won't get off scot-free,
   and God's loyal people will triumph.

²² Like a gold ring in a pig's snout
   is a beautiful face on an empty head.

²³ The desires of good people lead straight to the best,
   but wicked ambition ends in angry frustration.

²⁴ The world of the generous gets larger and larger;
   the world of the stingy gets smaller and smaller.

²⁵ The one who blesses others is abundantly blessed;
   those who help others are helped.

²⁶ Curses on those who drive a hard bargain!
   Blessings on all who play fair and square!

²⁷ The one who seeks good finds delight;
the student of evil becomes evil.

²⁸ A life devoted to things is a dead life, a stump;
a God-shaped life is a flourishing tree.

²⁹ Exploit or abuse your family, and end up with a fistful of air;
common sense tells you it's a stupid way to live.

³⁰ A good life is a fruit-bearing tree;
a violent life destroys souls.

³¹ If good people barely make it,
what's in store for the bad!

After the Passage

Have you ever thrown a rock into a still pond? The rock hits the water and sends ripples across the surface of the pond. The farther away they get from where the stone entered the water, the larger they get. The entire pond is changed, even if just for a moment, as a result of one stone entering the water. Similarly, our actions—wise or unwise—impact the world around us.

So much of the advice found in the book of Proverbs is intended to protect us from the results of foolish choices. In Proverbs 11, however, the emphasis is less on our personal well-being and more on the impact our choices have on others. We can almost hear Solomon say, "Have you stopped to consider how your actions will affect the people around you?" Our choices, wise or foolish, ripple beyond us to our immediate families and even to our communities and nations. This is another reason to prioritize wisdom—not simply for our own sake but for the sake of others.

Look at the puddle below to see how far our choices can reach.

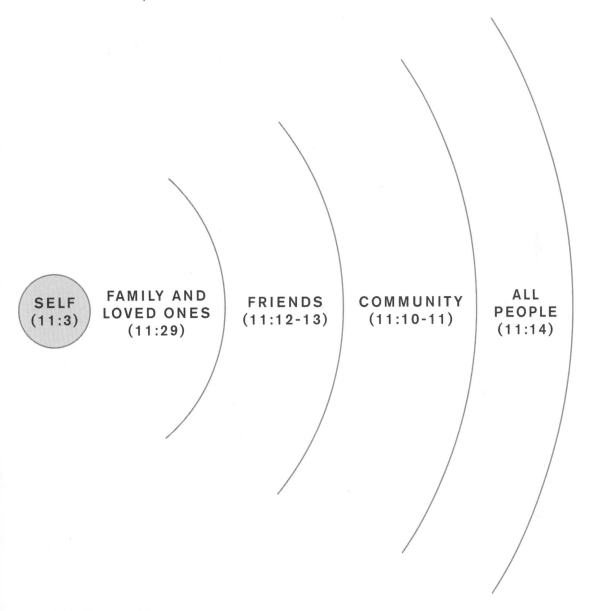

SELF
(11:3)

FAMILY AND
LOVED ONES
(11:29)

FRIENDS
(11:12-13)

COMMUNITY
(11:10-11)

ALL
PEOPLE
(11:14)

The Bottom Line

Our actions have ripple effects beyond what we may ever know.

EXPERIENCE

Think of a significant choice you've made recently. What was the impact of the choice? What might the impact have been if you had chosen differently?

THE IMPACT OF MY CHOICE	THE IMPACT OF A DIFFERENT CHOICE
on your family	on your family
on your friends	on your friends
on strangers	on strangers
on your neighborhood or community	on your neighborhood or community

Takeaway and Pray

My takeaway from this experience is

My prayer today is a

__ REQUEST __ CONFESSION __ PRAISE

calling stupid what it is

Proverbs 12

Know before You Go

The fool hates correction,
but the wise welcome
discipline.

Read the Passage

1 If you love learning, you love the discipline that goes with it—
   how shortsighted to refuse correction!

2 A good person basks in the delight of GOD,
   and he wants nothing to do with devious schemers.

3 You can't find firm footing in a swamp,
   but life rooted in God stands firm.

4 A hearty wife invigorates her husband,
   but a frigid woman is cancer in the bones.

⁵ The thinking of principled people makes for justice;
    the plots of degenerates corrupt.

⁶ The words of the wicked kill;
    the speech of the upright saves.

⁷ Wicked people fall to pieces—there's nothing to them;
    the homes of good people hold together.

⁸ A person who talks sense is honored;
    airheads are held in contempt.

⁹ Better to be ordinary and work for a living
    than act important and starve in the process.

¹⁰ Good people are good to their animals;
    the "good-hearted" bad people kick and abuse them.

¹¹ The one who stays on the job has food on the table;
    the witless chase whims and fancies.

¹² What the wicked construct finally falls into ruin,
    while the roots of the righteous give life, and more life.

¹³ The gossip of bad people gets them in trouble;
    the conversation of good people keeps them out of it.

¹⁴ Well-spoken words bring satisfaction;
    well-done work has its own reward.

¹⁵ Fools are headstrong and do what they like;
    wise people take advice.

[16] Fools have short fuses and explode all too quickly;
     the prudent quietly shrug off insults.

[17] Truthful witness by a good person clears the air,
     but liars lay down a smoke screen of deceit.

[18] Rash language cuts and maims,
     but there is healing in the words of the wise.

[19] Truth lasts;
     lies are here today, gone tomorrow.

[20] Evil scheming distorts the schemer;
     peace-planning brings joy to the planner.

[21] No evil can overwhelm a good person,
     but the wicked have their hands full of it.

[22] God can't stomach liars;
     he loves the company of those who keep their word.

[23] Prudent people don't flaunt their knowledge;
     talkative fools broadcast their silliness.

[24] The diligent find freedom in their work;
     the lazy are oppressed by work.

[25] Worry weighs us down;
     a cheerful word picks us up.

²⁶ A good person survives misfortune,
    but a wicked life invites disaster.

²⁷ A lazy life is an empty life,
    but "early to rise" gets the job done.

²⁸ Good men and women travel right into life;
    sin's detours take you straight to hell.

After the Passage

Most of the time, calling someone stupid is not a good idea. But Solomon isn't afraid to use strong language to describe foolish behavior. The strong language from Solomon throughout Proverbs—but particularly in chapter 12—demonstrates the importance of his advice.

If we are honest, we all typically try to avoid discipline because discipline usually hurts. Our perspective can shift, however, if we focus on the *purpose* of correction and discipline rather than the *pain* it brings. The purpose of wise correction is to help us avoid mistakes, become wiser, and live the lives God desires for us. Our parents, coaches, and teachers correct us so we can become the best versions of ourselves. The fool, however, does not understand the purpose of discipline and only sees the uncomfortable pain it brings. (Look back at reading 9 for more thoughts about receiving feedback and correction.)

Another theme emerges in Proverbs 12: the idea of honesty. Permanence and favor come with the truth. Look at Proverbs 12:17, 19, and 22. Think about your group of friends; your longest friendships are probably with people who have been honest with you over time. If you had a friend who continually lied to you, there's a good chance your friendship would not last very long. Dishonest people tend to move from group to group because eventually they break people's trust with their lies. People who lie have a hard time staying in leadership, on teams, or in relationships.

Solomon's advice about prioritizing honesty is related to the advice about receiving correction: When someone gives you honest feedback, even if it is difficult to hear, it is actually a good thing because it helps you grow as a person! A lie may feel good in the moment but will never help you see the areas in your life that need attention. In the long run, honesty is better for everyone.

The Bottom Line

Even when it hurts, honesty is better than lying.

EXPERIENCE

When was the last time someone lied to you? How did it make you feel?

What are some reasons people lie?

Is there anyone you've lied to recently? What can you do this week to make it right?

Solomon's instructions in Proverbs 12 are about more than just lying. There are a variety of ways to be dishonest beyond not telling the truth when someone asks you a question. Cheating, stealing, withholding information, and exaggerating are a few more examples of dishonesty.

Revisit the last question with this broader understanding of honesty and integrity in mind. Is there anyone you need to make things right with this week?

Takeaway and Pray

My takeaway from this experience is

My prayer today is a

__ REQUEST __ CONFESSION __ PRAISE

tool or treasure

Proverbs 13

Know before You Go

Solomon looks at the role money can play in our lives when we use it wisely or foolishly.

Read the Passage

¹ Intelligent children listen to their parents;
    foolish children do their own thing.

² The good acquire a taste for helpful conversation;
    bullies push and shove their way through life.

³ Careful words make for a careful life;
    careless talk may ruin everything.

⁴ Indolence wants it all and gets nothing;
    the energetic have something to show for their lives.

[5] A good person hates false talk;
  a bad person wallows in gibberish.

[6] A God-loyal life keeps you on track;
  sin dumps the wicked in the ditch.

[7] A pretentious, showy life is an empty life;
  a plain and simple life is a full life.

[8] The rich can be sued for everything they have,
  but the poor are free of such threats.

[9] The lives of good people are brightly lit streets;
  the lives of the wicked are dark alleys.

[10] Arrogant know-it-alls stir up discord,
  but wise men and women listen to each other's counsel.

[11] Easy come, easy go,
  but steady diligence pays off.

[12] Unrelenting disappointment leaves you heartsick,
  but a sudden good break can turn life around.

[13] Ignore the Word and suffer;
  honor God's commands and grow rich.

[14] The teaching of the wise is a fountain of life,
  so, no more drinking from death-tainted wells!

[15] Sound thinking makes for gracious living,
  but liars walk a rough road.

¹⁶ A commonsense person *lives* good sense;
    fools litter the country with silliness.

¹⁷ Irresponsible talk makes a real mess of things,
    but a reliable reporter is a healing presence.

¹⁸ Refuse discipline and end up homeless;
    embrace correction and live an honored life.

¹⁹ Souls who follow their hearts thrive;
    fools bent on evil despise matters of soul.

²⁰ Become wise by walking with the wise;
    hang out with fools and watch your life fall to pieces.

²¹ Disaster entraps sinners,
    but God-loyal people get a good life.

²² A good life gets passed on to the grandchildren;
    ill-gotten wealth ends up with good people.

²³ Banks foreclose on the farms of the poor,
    or else the poor lose their shirts to crooked lawyers.

²⁴ A refusal to correct is a refusal to love;
    love your children by disciplining them.

²⁵ An appetite for good brings much satisfaction,
    but the belly of the wicked always wants more.

After the Passage

We know Solomon was the wisest of all Israel's kings, but sometimes we forget that he was also the richest. He had everything money could buy. And yet he repeatedly warns us to be responsible with our money.

You may not have a lot of money right now. But you will someday. You may not have a lot of bills to pay or a budget and finances to manage, but you will. You may or may not have a job right now, but you will. Regardless of your current financial situation, it is important to start thinking about money wisely right now. The habits you establish when you're young will reap great rewards over time.

As Solomon explains, the minute obtaining more money becomes our primary goal, we've allowed it to become too important. A person who views money as a tool is wise; a person who allows money to become their treasure is foolish. Let's look at some proverbs that show differences in how the wise and the foolish use money.

PROVERB	THE WISE	THE FOOLISH
6:10-11		indulge in unproductive habits that can lead to a "dirt-poor life"
11:18	earn money honestly and are rewarded	earn money that does not last by cheating the system
11:28	trust in God more than in material wealth	trust in material wealth more than in God
13:18		resist discipline and experience financial hardship
13:22	prepare and save money for their families down the road	have nothing in the end because their wealth is given to the wise

The Bottom Line

Wise people view money as a tool; fools view money as treasure.

EXPERIENCE

Think about your friends. Do they talk about money as tool or treasure? Pay attention to that this week.

If you are someone who spends your money as soon as you get it, try tucking some away this week. Then you'll be using money as a tool to develop self-control.

If you are someone who never spends money and tends to hoard it, try blessing someone this week in a way that costs you money. Then you'll be using your money as a tool to develop generosity and open-handedness.

Takeaway and Pray

My takeaway from this experience is

My prayer today is a

__ **REQUEST** __ **CONFESSION** __ **PRAISE**

movie trailers for your heart

Proverbs 14

Know before You Go

Proverbs 14 shows how the words we say are a direct reflection of the condition of our hearts.

Read the Passage

¹ Lady Wisdom builds a lovely home;
  Sir Fool comes along and tears it down brick by brick.

² An honest life shows respect for GOD;
  a degenerate life is a slap in his face.

³ Frivolous talk provokes a derisive smile;
  wise speech evokes nothing but respect.

⁴ No cattle, no crops;
  a good harvest requires a strong ox for the plow.

⁵ A true witness never lies;
  a false witness makes a business of it.

⁶ Cynics look high and low for wisdom—and never find it;
　　the open-minded find it right on their doorstep!

⁷ Escape quickly from the company of fools;
　　they're a waste of your time, a waste of your words.

⁸ The wisdom of the wise keeps life on track;
　　the foolishness of fools lands them in the ditch.

⁹ The stupid ridicule right and wrong,
　　but a moral life is a favored life.

¹⁰ The person who shuns the bitter moments of friends
　　will be an outsider at their celebrations.

¹¹ Lives of careless wrongdoing are run-down shacks;
　　holy living builds soaring cathedrals.

¹²⁻¹³ There's a way of life that looks harmless enough;
　　look again—it leads straight to hell.
　Sure, those people appear to be having a good time,
　　but all that laughter will end in heartbreak.

¹⁴ A mean person gets paid back in meanness,
　　a gracious person in grace.

¹⁵ The gullible believe anything they're told;
　　the prudent sift and weigh every word.

¹⁶ The wise watch their steps and avoid evil;
　　fools are headstrong and reckless.

[17] The hotheaded do things they'll later regret;
 the coldhearted get the cold shoulder.

[18] Foolish dreamers live in a world of illusion;
 wise realists plant their feet on the ground.

[19] Eventually, evil will pay tribute to good;
 the wicked will respect God-loyal people.

[20] An unlucky loser is shunned by all,
 but everyone loves a winner.

[21] It's criminal to ignore a neighbor in need,
 but compassion for the poor—what a blessing!

[22] Isn't it obvious that conspirators lose out,
 while the thoughtful win love and trust?

[23] Hard work always pays off;
 mere talk puts no bread on the table.

[24] The wise accumulate wisdom;
 fools get stupider by the day.

[25] Souls are saved by truthful witness
 and betrayed by the spread of lies.

[26] The Fear-of-GOD builds up confidence,
 and makes a world safe for your children.

[27] The Fear-of-GOD is a spring of living water
 so you won't go off drinking from poisoned wells.

28 The mark of a good leader is loyal followers;
    leadership is nothing without a following.

29 Slowness to anger makes for deep understanding;
    a quick-tempered person stockpiles stupidity.

30 A sound mind makes for a robust body,
    but runaway emotions corrode the bones.

31 You insult your Maker when you exploit the powerless;
    when you're kind to the poor, you honor God.

32 The evil of bad people leaves them out in the cold;
    the integrity of good people creates a safe place for living.

33 Lady Wisdom is at home in an understanding heart—
    fools never even get to say hello.

34 God-devotion makes a country strong;
    God-avoidance leaves people weak.

35 Diligent work gets a warm commendation;
    shiftless work earns an angry rebuke.

After the Passage

A movie trailer foreshadows a movie's action, drama, failures, and victories. Just by watching a good two-minute trailer, you can tell what kind of movie to expect and whether or not it's worth seeing. The things we say during the day are like movie trailers for our hearts. The book of Proverbs talks a great deal about the way we speak.

By this point in Proverbs, you have probably noticed that entire chapters are not typically focused on one specific topic. Instead, chapters are full of short, two-line pieces of advice. In addition to the advice found in Proverbs 14, Solomon sprinkles in proverbs about our speech all over the book. Take a look at just a few of these examples:

- 11:9: "The loose tongue of the godless spreads destruction."

- 15:1: "A gentle response defuses anger, but a sharp tongue kindles a temper-fire."

- 15:4: "Kind words heal and help; cutting words wound and maim."

- 16:24: "Gracious speech is like clover honey—good taste to the soul, quick energy for the body."

- 18:4: "Many words rush along like rivers in flood."

- 18:20: "Words satisfy the mind as much as fruit does the stomach; good talk is as gratifying as a good harvest."

The Bottom Line

Our words are a reflection of what is in our hearts.

EXPERIENCE

Take an honest look at the words that come out of your mouth. Are they crude? Kind? Angry? Argumentative? Caring? Positive? Negative? Reflect on your words over each of the next five days. Select a word for each day that describes the kind of things you tend to say.

Day one:

Day two:

Day three:

Day four:

Day five:

Takeaway and Pray

My takeaway from this experience is

My prayer today is a

__ REQUEST __ CONFESSION __ PRAISE

who stole the cookies from the cookie jar?

Proverbs 15

Know before You Go

Solomon explains that God sees our hearts.

Read the Passage

¹ A gentle response defuses anger,
   but a sharp tongue kindles a temper-fire.

² Knowledge flows like spring water from the wise;
   fools are leaky faucets, dripping nonsense.

³ GOD doesn't miss a thing—
   he's alert to good and evil alike.

⁴ Kind words heal and help;
   cutting words wound and maim.

⁵ Moral dropouts won't listen to their elders;
   welcoming correction is a mark of good sense.

[6] The lives of God-loyal people flourish;
    a misspent life is soon bankrupt.

[7] Perceptive words spread knowledge;
    fools are hollow—there's nothing to them.

[8] GOD can't stand pious poses,
    but he delights in genuine prayers.

[9] A life frittered away disgusts GOD;
    he loves those who run straight for the finish line.

[10] It's a school of hard knocks for those who leave God's path,
    a dead-end street for those who hate God's rules.

[11] Even hell holds no secrets from GOD—
    do you think he can't read human hearts?

[12] Know-it-alls don't like being told what to do;
    they avoid the company of wise men and women.

[13] A cheerful heart brings a smile to your face;
    a sad heart makes it hard to get through the day.

[14] An intelligent person is always eager to take in more truth;
    fools feed on fast-food fads and fancies.

[15] A miserable heart means a miserable life;
    a cheerful heart fills the day with song.

[16] A simple life in the Fear-of-GOD
    is better than a rich life with a ton of headaches.

¹⁷ Better a bread crust shared in love
    than a slab of prime rib served in hate.

¹⁸ Hot tempers start fights;
    a calm, cool spirit keeps the peace.

¹⁹ The path of lazy people is overgrown with briers;
    the diligent walk down a smooth road.

²⁰ Intelligent children make their parents proud;
    lazy students embarrass their parents.

²¹ The empty-headed treat life as a plaything;
    the perceptive grasp its meaning and make a go of it.

²² Refuse good advice and watch your plans fail;
    take good counsel and watch them succeed.

²³ Congenial conversation—what a pleasure!
    The right word at the right time—beautiful!

²⁴ Life ascends to the heights for the thoughtful—
    it's a clean about-face from descent into hell.

²⁵ GOD smashes the pretensions of the arrogant;
    he stands with those who have no standing.

²⁶ GOD can't stand evil scheming,
    but he puts words of grace and beauty on display.

²⁷ A greedy and grasping person destroys community;
    those who refuse to exploit live and let live.

²⁸ Prayerful answers come from God-loyal people;
   the wicked are sewers of abuse.

²⁹ GOD keeps his distance from the wicked;
   he closely attends to the prayers of God-loyal people.

³⁰ A twinkle in the eye means joy in the heart,
   and good news makes you feel fit as a fiddle.

³¹ Listen to good advice if you want to live well,
   an honored guest among wise men and women.

³² An undisciplined, self-willed life is puny;
   an obedient, God-willed life is spacious.

³³ Fear-of-GOD is a school in skilled living—
   first you learn humility, then you experience glory.

After the Passage

Solomon focuses a lot on wise and foolish actions, but we should not forget that our actions reflect something much deeper: our hearts. Your heart is the source of all your actions, and Solomon reminds us that God's watchful eye sees directly into every wise and wicked heart.

Imagine a child, close to dinnertime, being tempted by a jar full of warm chocolate chip cookies. He sneaks into the kitchen when no one is around and eats the entire batch. He is certain that he will get away with it—no one is in the room when he does it. But there are crumbs on the floor, an empty cookie jar with the lid still off, and chocolate smeared across his face.

When the boy's mother asks him if he ate the cookies, he shakes his head no. He assumes his mom couldn't possibly know what he has done. He assumes wrong.

As silly as this example is, when we try to hide our sin from God, we look just as ridiculous. In Proverbs 15:3, Solomon reminds us that God sees everything—both good and evil. While for some this may be a scary thought, for those living a wise life, this is comforting. Just as God sees the wicked, He also sees the righteous!

The Bottom Line

We cannot hide our hearts from God.

EXPERIENCE

Read Psalm 139:23-24 and Psalm 51:7-15. These words are attributed to Solomon's father, King David, who is one of Israel's most famous kings. David is remembered for having a heart for God, yet he made some terrible decisions that had horrible consequences. In these psalms we see David pleading with God to make his heart pure. He understood that in order to change his actions he had to first change his heart. And in order for his heart to change, he needed God's help!

Spend five minutes in silence. Ask God to reveal anything in your heart that doesn't honor Him.

After five minutes in silence, confess to God any sinful behavior or desire in your heart that He has revealed to you. Ask God for forgiveness and a pure heart.

GOD ALREADY
KNOWS EVERYTHING
ABOUT YOU—EVEN
YOUR SECRETS.

This exercise may be uncomfortable for you. We often have a difficult time being still and silent. This practice, however, allows us to quiet down and slow down enough to really consider the state of our hearts. It's very difficult to do that kind of reflection when you are busy and active.

It can be scary to admit things in your life that you are not proud of. But remember that God already knows everything about you—even your secrets. Confessing to God is a great way to acknowledge your sin and turn away from its patterns in your life.

Takeaway and Pray

My takeaway from this experience is

My prayer today is a

__ REQUEST   __ CONFESSION   __ PRAISE

kings and things

Proverbs 16

Know before You Go

Solomon describes God as the ultimate King.

Read the Passage

¹ Mortals make elaborate plans,
   but GOD has the last word.

² Humans are satisfied with whatever looks good;
   GOD probes for what *is* good.

³ Put GOD in charge of your work,
   then what you've planned will take place.

⁴ GOD made everything with a place and purpose;
   even the wicked are included—but for *judgment.*

⁵ GOD can't stomach arrogance or pretense;
    believe me, he'll put those braggarts in their place.

⁶ Guilt is banished through love and truth;
    Fear-of-GOD deflects evil.

⁷ When GOD approves of your life,
    even your enemies will end up shaking your hand.

⁸ Far better to be right and poor
    than to be wrong and rich.

⁹ We plan the way we want to live,
    but only GOD makes us able to live it.

¹⁰ A good leader motivates,
    doesn't mislead, doesn't exploit.

¹¹ GOD cares about honesty in the workplace;
    your business is his business.

¹² Good leaders abhor wrongdoing of all kinds;
    sound leadership has a moral foundation.

¹³ Good leaders cultivate honest speech;
    they love advisors who tell them the truth.

¹⁴ An intemperate leader wreaks havoc in lives;
    you're smart to stay clear of someone like that.

¹⁵ Good-tempered leaders invigorate lives;
    they're like spring rain and sunshine.

¹⁶ Get wisdom—it's worth more than money;
    choose insight over income every time.

¹⁷ The road of right living bypasses evil;
    watch your step and save your life.

¹⁸ First pride, then the crash—
    the bigger the ego, the harder the fall.

¹⁹ It's better to live humbly among the poor
    than to live it up among the rich and famous.

²⁰ It pays to take life seriously;
    things work out when you trust in GOD.

²¹ A wise person gets known for insight;
    gracious words add to one's reputation.

²² True intelligence is a spring of fresh water,
    while fools sweat it out the hard way.

²³ They make a lot of sense, these wise folks;
    whenever they speak, their reputation increases.

²⁴ Gracious speech is like clover honey—
    good taste to the soul, quick energy for the body.

²⁵ There's a way that looks harmless enough;
    look again—it leads straight to hell.

²⁶ Appetite is an incentive to work;
    hunger makes you work all the harder.

²⁷ Mean people spread mean gossip;
　　their words smart and burn.

²⁸ Troublemakers start fights;
　　gossips break up friendships.

²⁹ Calloused climbers betray their very own friends;
　　they'd stab their own grandmothers in the back.

³⁰ A shifty eye betrays an evil intention;
　　a clenched jaw signals trouble ahead.

³¹ Gray hair is a mark of distinction,
　　the award for a God-loyal life.

³² Moderation is better than muscle,
　　self-control better than political power.

³³ Make your motions and cast your votes,
　　but GOD has the final say.

After the Passage

There are two major themes in Proverbs 16:

1. God is in control of every aspect of our lives! Read Proverbs 16:1-4 again. Notice how Solomon elevates God's plans and desires over humans' plans and desires.

2. There is no place for the arrogant in the Kingdom of God.

Perhaps you have allowed yourself to dream about what it would be like to be a king, queen, or president. The ability to do whatever you'd like, whenever you'd like, is very appealing! While many of us will never experience that type of power or authority, we all face the temptation to be kings and queens of our own lives. Children may respond to instructions from parents or teachers by saying, "No! I can do it myself!" or "You can't make me!" We are tempted to run our lives, our little kingdoms, as if we call the shots.

Unfortunately, we do not necessarily grow out of this stubbornness. We may no longer throw temper tantrums or scream at those in authority over us, but we certainly still desire to live our lives the way we want to live our lives. We want to do what feels good, what causes us the least trouble, and what benefits us the most. *Forgive my friend who hurt me? You can't make me! Don't look at this or that on my phone? But I want to! Don't gossip or tease a classmate? We are just having fun—let me do it! Sacrifice some of my hard-earned money or some of my precious time to serve someone? No way—my friends are not spending their time or money that way!* The list could go on and on. We never grow out of wanting to run our lives.

Remembering that God is ultimately in control will help keep us humble. It is *God* who is over all. In fact, that is how Proverbs 16 ends (see Proverbs 16:33). Even the most powerful person in the world needs God's help, wisdom, and guidance. It doesn't matter if you are a team captain, president of your class, the oldest child in your family, or one day the president of a company: You will never outrank God!

The Bottom Line

We should be careful not to think of ourselves too highly. God is the One who rules over all.

EXPERIENCE

When you think about the various categories of your life, in what ways do you think your plans might differ from God's plans for you?

MY PLANS FOR MY LIFE	GOD'S PLANS FOR MY LIFE

Pray this simple prayer:

God, help me get out of the way today and do whatever you would have me do. Help me see people the way you see them. Help me give thanks for the opportunities you give me. Help me honor you with the decisions I make today. Amen.

Takeaway and Pray

My takeaway from this experience is

My prayer today is a

__ REQUEST __ CONFESSION __ PRAISE

fights, follow-through, and family

Proverbs 17

Know before You Go

King Solomon shares the importance of wisdom and how it benefits us at every stage of life.

Read the Passage

¹ A meal of bread and water in contented peace
    is better than a banquet spiced with quarrels.

² A wise servant takes charge of an unruly child
    and is honored as one of the family.

³ As silver in a crucible and gold in a pan,
    so our lives are refined by GOD.

⁴ Evil people relish malicious conversation;
    the ears of liars itch for dirty gossip.

[5] Whoever mocks poor people insults their Creator;
     gloating over misfortune is a punishable crime.

[6] Old people are distinguished by grandchildren;
     children take pride in their parents.

[7] We don't expect eloquence from fools,
     nor do we expect lies from our leaders.

[8] Receiving a gift is like getting a rare gemstone;
     any way you look at it, you see beauty refracted.

[9] Overlook an offense and bond a friendship;
     fasten on to a slight and—good-bye, friend!

[10] A quiet rebuke to a person of good sense
     does more than a whack on the head of a fool.

[11] Criminals out looking for nothing but trouble
     won't have to wait long—they'll meet it coming and going!

[12] Better to meet a grizzly robbed of her cubs
     than a fool hellbent on folly.

[13] Those who return evil for good
     will meet their own evil returning.

[14] The start of a quarrel is like a leak in a dam,
     so stop it before it bursts.

[15] Whitewashing bad people and throwing mud on good people
     are equally abhorrent to GOD.

16 What's this? Fools out shopping for wisdom!
    They wouldn't recognize it if they saw it!

17 Friends love through all kinds of weather,
    and families stick together in all kinds of trouble.

18 It's stupid to try to get something for nothing,
    or run up huge bills you can never pay.

19 The person who courts sin marries trouble;
    build a wall, invite a burglar.

20 A bad motive can't achieve a good end;
    double-talk brings you double trouble.

21 Having a fool for a child is misery;
    it's no fun being the parent of a dolt.

22 A cheerful disposition is good for your health;
    gloom and doom leave you bone-tired.

23 The wicked take bribes under the table;
    they show nothing but contempt for justice.

24 The perceptive find wisdom in their own front yard;
    fools look for it everywhere but right here.

25 A surly, stupid child is sheer pain to a father,
    a bitter pill for a mother to swallow.

26 It's wrong to penalize good behavior,
    or make good citizens pay for the crimes of others.

²⁷ The one who knows much says little;
　　an understanding person remains calm.

²⁸ Even dunces who keep quiet are thought to be wise;
　　as long as they keep their mouths shut, they're smart.

After the Passage

Solomon explained the power of words in Proverbs 14, but we often need reminders that will make ideas stick in our minds. In Proverbs 17, Solomon reiterates that our words have deep roots running down directly to our hearts. The source of our words distinguishes what type of people we are—either foolish or wise. In fact, Solomon mentions some specific ways our words can affect our lives and relationships:

Our words can cause fighting (Proverbs 17:14, 19): Words are sharp. Sometimes our words can be so damaging that they lead to fighting. Solomon uses the picture of a dam bursting open in Proverbs 17:14 to describe how quickly our words can escalate things. The fool does not know how to control their word flow before the dam breaks! Proverbs 17:20 adds another layer to this: People who try to manipulate with their words bring trouble on themselves. That's some pretty strong language!

Our words can promise what we can't deliver (Proverbs 17:18): We usually have good intentions, but sometimes we agree to things we cannot follow through on later. Proverbs 17:18 describes how fools commits to things without knowing whether they will be able to keep their end of the bargain. Realizing that they spoke too soon, they back out later. Wise people never commit without thinking of possible outcomes or the responsibility a commitment might require. If they do make a commitment, wise people stick with it to the end.

Our words can injure our families (Proverbs 17:6, 25): Think about the people closest to you. For many, this will be family. They see the true you more than anyone else. When it comes to our words, our parents get both our best and our worst.

In fact, they were probably there for the first words we ever spoke! Parents love their children, and grandparents love their grandchildren (Proverbs 17:6), but while the words of a wise child bring extra happiness and joy, a foolish child can deeply injure their relationship with their family (Proverbs 17:25). Do your words make your family joyful or miserable at home?

The Bottom Line

Words are powerful! They expose our foolishness and our wisdom.

EXPERIENCE

Our words can cause fighting. Read Proverbs 17:14 again and think about the last fight you had. Were your words wise or unwise? What impact did your words have?

WORDS I USED	THE IMPACT OF MY WORDS

Our words can promise what we can't deliver. Read Proverbs 17:18 again. In what ways might promising to do something you won't be able to follow through on be foolish? Give an example from your own experience.

Our words can injure our families. Being wise at home is harder than being wise in public. What types of words do you typically use at home—wise, joyful words or sharp, foolish words? Reflect on a time when your words brought joy to your family and a time when they brought sadness or hurt.

WORDS I SAID THAT BROUGHT JOY TO MY FAMILY	WORDS I SAID THAT BROUGHT SADNESS OR HURT TO MY FAMILY

Takeaway and Pray

My takeaway from this experience is

My prayer today is a

___ REQUEST ___ CONFESSION ___ PRAISE

listen, speak, repeat

Proverbs 18

Know before You Go

Solomon discusses the wisdom of listening.

Read the Passage

¹ Loners who care only for themselves
    spit on the common good.

² Fools care nothing for thoughtful discourse;
    all they do is run off at the mouth.

³ When wickedness arrives, shame's not far behind;
    contempt for life is contemptible.

⁴ Many words rush along like rivers in flood,
    but deep wisdom flows up from artesian springs.

⁵ It's not right to go easy on the guilty,
  or come down hard on the innocent.

⁶ The words of a fool start fights;
  do him a favor and gag him.

⁷ Fools are undone by their big mouths;
  their souls are crushed by their words.

⁸ Listening to gossip is like eating cheap candy;
  do you really want junk like that in your belly?

⁹ Slack habits and sloppy work
  are as bad as vandalism.

¹⁰ GOD's name is a place of protection—
  good people can run there and be safe.

¹¹ The rich think their wealth protects them;
  they imagine themselves safe behind it.

¹² Pride first, then the crash,
  but humility is precursor to honor.

¹³ Answering before listening
  is both stupid and rude.

¹⁴ A healthy spirit conquers adversity,
  but what can you do when the spirit is crushed?

¹⁵ Wise men and women are always learning,
  always listening for fresh insights.

¹⁶ A gift gets attention;
  it buys the attention of eminent people.

¹⁷ The first speech in a court case is always convincing—
  until the cross-examination starts!

¹⁸ You may have to draw straws
  when faced with a tough decision.

¹⁹ Do a favor and win a friend forever;
  nothing can untie that bond.

²⁰ Words satisfy the mind as much as fruit does the stomach;
  good talk is as gratifying as a good harvest.

²¹ Words kill, words give life;
  they're either poison or fruit—you choose.

²² Find a good spouse, you find a good life—
  and even more: the favor of God!

²³ The poor speak in soft supplications;
  the rich bark out answers.

²⁴ Friends come and friends go,
  but a true friend sticks by you like family.

After the Passage

When we think of wise people, we often think of people who give good advice. And while we have already seen that our words are indeed a good indicator of our wisdom, it turns out that knowing when *not* to talk is also a great indicator of it!

Giving sound advice is important, but so is listening well. In Proverbs 18, Solomon underscores the importance of not rushing to speak. For instance, in Proverbs 18:2, Solomon explains that fools have no desire to learn or gain understanding. Rather, they love to share their opinions, even if they are not particularly well informed.

Solomon has some very strong language about the words (or mouths) of fools in Proverbs 18:6-7. The words of fools are traps that bring about grief and strife. Once again, the importance of speaking wisely—or not speaking at all—is extremely important.

Read Proverbs 18:13 again. Solomon highlights the foolishness of speaking before listening because it is difficult to understand a situation or a person if we are simply trying to insert our own opinions into the conversation. Have you ever witnessed someone who wished they could take back something they said after they learned the full picture? Listening is an important skill that leads to a life of wisdom.

Listening has very specific practical benefits. Listening before you jump to conclusions helps build patience, which is always a great trait to possess! Listening also helps you build trust and relationships with your friends and family because you will earn the reputation of someone who is approachable, caring, and interested in other people's lives. Listening well also eliminates the wasted time and energy that come with trying to solve a problem that you do not fully understand. Last, listening well helps broaden your perspective: You learn a great deal when you listen! Solomon's counsel to listen first and speak second is indeed great advice.

The Bottom Line

A wise person listens first and speaks second.

EXPERIENCE

Who is the best listener in your life? In the next week, thank this person for being a wise person and a great listener.

Practice good listening this week by trying to do the following in your conversations:

- Commit to not interrupting your conversation partner.
- Ask a follow-up question when someone has finished sharing.
- Give your opinion only when asked.
- Ask your friends at least one open-ended question (as opposed to a yes-or-no question) every day. For instance, "How do you feel about this thing that happened?" or "What about this situation makes you sad/excited/frustrated?"
- Set your phone aside while you're talking to someone so it won't distract you. Consider how you can limit other distractions as well.

What did you learn this week as you listened well?

Takeaway and Pray

My takeaway from this experience is

My prayer today is a

__ REQUEST __ CONFESSION __ PRAISE

the struggle is real

Proverbs 19

Know before You Go

Solomon introduces two types of poverty.

Read the Passage

¹ Better to be poor and honest
than a rich person no one can trust.

² Ignorant zeal is worthless;
haste makes waste.

³ People ruin their lives by their own stupidity,
so why does GOD always get blamed?

⁴ Wealth attracts friends as honey draws flies,
but poor people are avoided like a plague.

⁵ Perjury won't go unpunished.
Would you let a liar go free?

⁶ Lots of people flock around a generous person;
    everyone's a friend to the philanthropist.

⁷ When you're down on your luck, even your family avoids you—
    yes, even your best friends wish you'd get lost.
  If they see you coming, they look the other way—
    out of sight, out of mind.

⁸ Grow a wise heart—you'll do yourself a favor;
    keep a clear head—you'll find a good life.

⁹ The person who tells lies gets caught;
    the person who spreads rumors is ruined.

¹⁰ Blockheads shouldn't live on easy street
    any more than workers should give orders to their boss.

¹¹ Smart people know how to hold their tongue;
    their grandeur is to forgive and forget.

¹² Mean-tempered leaders are like mad dogs;
    the good-natured are like fresh morning dew.

¹³ A parent is worn to a frazzle by an irresponsible child;
    a nagging spouse is a leaky faucet.

¹⁴ House and land are handed down from parents,
    but a congenial spouse comes straight from GOD.

¹⁵ Life collapses on loafers;
    lazybones go hungry.

¹⁶ Keep the rules and keep your life;
  careless living kills.

¹⁷ Mercy to the needy is a loan to GOD,
  and GOD pays back those loans in full.

¹⁸ Discipline your children while you still have the chance;
  indulging them destroys them.

¹⁹ Let angry people endure the backlash of their own anger;
  if you try to make it better, you'll only make it worse.

²⁰ Take good counsel and accept correction—
  that's the way to live wisely and well.

²¹ We humans keep brainstorming options and plans,
  but GOD's purpose prevails.

²² It's only human to want to make a buck,
  but it's better to be poor than a liar.

²³ Fear-of-GOD is life itself,
  a full life, and serene—no nasty surprises.

²⁴ Some people dig a fork into the pie
  but are too lazy to raise it to their mouth.

²⁵ Punish the insolent—make an example of them.
  Who knows? Somebody might learn a good lesson.

²⁶ Kids who lash out against their parents
  are an embarrassment and disgrace.

27 If you quit listening, dear child, and strike off on your own,
   you'll soon be out of your depth.

28 An unprincipled witness desecrates justice;
   the mouths of the wicked spew malice.

29 The irreverent have to learn reverence the hard way;
   only a slap in the face brings fools to attention.

After the Passage

When you think of poverty, what comes to mind? Unfortunately, there is no shortage of images to think about. Poverty existed in Solomon's day just as much as it exists now. In Proverbs 19, Solomon talks about the very real struggle of the poor and gives insight for how to avoid poverty and how to care for those who are struggling. While poverty can happen for lots of reasons, Proverbs 19 highlights two of the main factors contributing to poverty:

- things we do
- things outside our control (including things other people do)

Solomon links the first type of poverty (things we do) to foolishness. Failure and loss come to people "by their own stupidity" (Proverbs 19:3)—through rushed decisions, dishonesty, ignorance, and the like. Foolish people doing foolish things have a hard time holding on to wealth; they often lose money. Later, in Proverbs 19:15, Solomon ties poverty to laziness. Many who find themselves in poverty have not worked hard to support themselves.

Solomon is much more gentle with people stuck in the second type of poverty. Even the wisest people may find themselves struggling with things outside their control. For example, a parent may get laid off from work, an ill grandparent may face expensive medical bills, a child may be born into an impoverished situation, or a family may experience a natural disaster. Solomon realizes that life can be very harsh and instructs us to care for the poor. When we help the poor who struggle, it is like giving directly to God. In fact, God even rewards helpers because their work shows love for a person He loves too (Proverbs 19:17).

The Bottom Line

Poverty is sometimes the result of things we do, but it can also come from things outside our control.

EXPERIENCE

Think about the last show you watched or book you read where poverty was a theme. Was the cause something the characters did or something outside their control? How was their poverty treated in the story?

While we can't always avoid poverty that comes from forces outside our control, what are some ways that foolish choices could lead to poverty?

Think of your habits and choices you make regularly. Could any of them contribute to a life of poverty for you down the road?

Read Proverbs 19:17 again. How can you show care for poor people in your community? Write down some things you've done recently that have shown care for someone in need, and then write down a prayer for that person.

Takeaway and Pray

My takeaway from this experience is

My prayer today is a

___ REQUEST ___ CONFESSION ___ PRAISE

chip scams and honest scales

Proverbs 20

Know before You Go

Solomon shows us that God rules with love, justice, and honesty.

Read the Passage

¹ Wine makes you mean, beer makes you quarrelsome—
   a staggering drunk is not much fun.

² Quick-tempered leaders are like mad dogs—
   cross them and they bite your head off.

³ It's a mark of good character to avert quarrels,
   but fools love to pick fights.

⁴ A farmer too lazy to plant in the spring
   has nothing to harvest in the fall.

⁵ Knowing what is right is like deep water in the heart;
   a wise person draws from the well within.

⁶ Lots of people claim to be loyal and loving,
  but where on earth can you find one?

⁷ Go-loyal people, living honest lives,
  make it much easier for their children.

⁸⁻⁹ Leaders who know their business and care
  keep a sharp eye out for the shoddy and cheap,
For who among us can be trusted
  to be always diligent and honest?

¹⁰ Switching price tags and padding the expense account
  are two things GOD hates.

¹¹ Young people eventually reveal by their actions
  if their motives are on the up and up.

¹² Ears that hear and eyes that see—
  we get our basic equipment from GOD!

¹³ Don't be too fond of sleep; you'll end up in the poorhouse.
  Wake up and get up; then there'll be food on the table.

¹⁴ The shopper says, "That's junk—I'll take it off your hands,"
  then goes off boasting of the bargain.

¹⁵ Drinking from the beautiful chalice of knowledge
  is better than adorning oneself with gold and rare gems.

¹⁶ Hold tight to collateral on any loan to a stranger;
  beware of accepting what a transient has pawned.

[17] Stolen bread tastes sweet,
     but soon your mouth is full of gravel.

[18] Form your purpose by asking for counsel,
     then carry it out using all the help you can get.

[19] Gossips can't keep secrets,
     so never confide in blabbermouths.

[20] Anyone who curses father and mother
     extinguishes light and exists benighted.

[21] A bonanza at the beginning
     is no guarantee of blessing at the end.

[22] Don't ever say, "I'll get you for that!"
     Wait for GOD; he'll settle the score.

[23] GOD hates cheating in the marketplace;
     rigged scales are an outrage.

[24] The very steps we take come from GOD;
     otherwise how would we know where we're going?

[25] An impulsive vow is a trap;
     later you'll wish you could get out of it.

[26] After careful scrutiny, a wise leader
     makes a clean sweep of rebels and dolts.

[27] GOD is in charge of human life,
     watching and examining us inside and out.

²⁸ Love and truth form a good leader;
　　　sound leadership is founded on loving integrity.

²⁹ Youth may be admired for vigor,
　　　but gray hair gives prestige to old age.

³⁰ A good thrashing purges evil;
　　　punishment goes deep within us.

After the Passage

Have you ever bought a bag of your favorite chips and opened it only to find that the bag was half filled with air? Beyond being disappointed that you have fewer chips to enjoy than you originally thought, you may have also been frustrated, feeling like you were tricked into paying for more than what you got. This is similar to the image that Solomon uses in Proverbs 20 when talking about fair and false judgments.

In Solomon's day, the true value of something was put to the test by its weight. Sometimes merchants in the marketplace tried to trick their customers by shifting the weights on the scales so buyers would have to pay more money for the same items. This made the numbers on the scales inaccurate, giving a false judgment of an item's true value. The merchant would cheat the system, and the buyer would walk away paying a much higher price than the item was worth (see Proverbs 20:23).

Sound familiar? This practice is similar to the one that led to our half-empty bag of chips. Solomon uses this practice to highlight how God hates unfair judgments. Proverbs 20:10 says that God hates financial cheating. He wants us to reflect His justice and love. We should not be like the chip makers or the ancient merchants; we should use honest scales to make honest judgments.

Some Bible translations use the word *winnow* to describe the "clean sweep" of foolishness and evil that wise people engage in (see Proverbs 20:26). Winnowing is what a farmer would do to separate good grain from its outer covering, or chaff—a burst of air would blow away the chaff while the good, weightier grain would settle back into place. In Proverbs 20:8 and 26 we see that a wise person (and God Himself) can judge what is right and wrong, wicked and righteous, wise and foolish, by evaluating fairly and honestly.

The Bottom Line

God rules fairly in justice and love, and He asks us to do the same.

EXPERIENCE

Is there anyone in your life you have judged unfairly? Make a point this week to apologize to them.

How can the following factors lead to judging people wrongly?

- jumping to conclusions

- misunderstandings

- jealousy

- peer pressure

Takeaway and Pray

My takeaway from this experience is

My prayer today is a

__ REQUEST __ CONFESSION __ PRAISE

you can't outwise God

Proverbs 21

Know before You Go

Solomon reminds us that human wisdom never gains the victory over God's plans. God's wisdom is greater.

Read the Passage

¹ Good leadership is a channel of water controlled by GOD;
    he directs it to whatever ends he chooses.

² We justify our actions by appearances;
    GOD examines our motives.

³ Clean living before God and justice with our neighbors
    mean far more to GOD than religious performance.

⁴ Arrogance and pride—distinguishing marks in the wicked—
    are just plain sin.

⁵ Careful planning puts you ahead in the long run;
    hurry and scurry puts you further behind.

⁶ Make it to the top by lying and cheating;
      get paid with smoke and a promotion—to death!

⁷ The wicked get buried alive by their loot
      because they refuse to use it to help others.

⁸ Mixed motives twist life into tangles;
      pure motives take you straight down the road.

⁹ Better to live alone in a tumbledown shack
      than share a mansion with a nagging spouse.

¹⁰ Wicked souls love to make trouble;
      they feel nothing for friends and neighbors.

¹¹ Simpletons only learn the hard way,
      but the wise learn by listening.

¹² A God-loyal person will see right through the wicked
      and undo the evil they've planned.

¹³ If you stop your ears to the cries of the poor,
      your cries will go unheard, unanswered.

¹⁴ A quietly given gift soothes an irritable person;
      a heartfelt present cools a hot temper.

¹⁵ Good people celebrate when justice triumphs,
      but for the workers of evil it's a bad day.

¹⁶ Whoever wanders off the straight and narrow
      ends up in a congregation of ghosts.

¹⁷ You're addicted to thrills? What an empty life!
    The pursuit of pleasure is never satisfied.

¹⁸ What a bad person plots against the good, boomerangs;
    the plotter gets it in the end.

¹⁹ Better to live in a tent in the wild
    than with a cross and petulant spouse.

²⁰ Valuables are safe in a wise person's home;
    fools put it all out for yard sales.

²¹ Whoever goes hunting for what is right and kind
    finds life itself—*glorious* life!

²² One sage entered a whole city of armed soldiers—
    their trusted defenses fell to pieces!

²³ Watch your words and hold your tongue;
    you'll save yourself a lot of grief.

²⁴ You know their names—Brash, Impudent, Blasphemer—
    intemperate hotheads, every one.

²⁵ Lazy people finally die of hunger
    because they won't get up and go to work.

²⁶ Sinners are always wanting what they don't have;
    the God-loyal are always giving what they do have.

²⁷ Religious performance by the wicked stinks;
    it's even worse when they use it to get ahead.

²⁸ A lying witness is unconvincing;
      a person who speaks truth is respected.

²⁹ Unscrupulous people fake it a lot;
      honest people are sure of their steps.

³⁰ Nothing clever, nothing conceived, nothing contrived,
      can get the better of GOD.

³¹ Do your best, prepare for the worst—
      then trust GOD to bring victory.

After the Passage

Proverbs 21 is full of contrasting statements. *The evil do this . . . but the righteous do that. The fool loves this . . . but the wise love that.* Most of these statements are centered on the differences between what we plan and desire for ourselves and what God plans and desires for us. The fool (or the wicked person) is consistently portrayed as someone who prioritizes short-term gain and selfish desires; someone who neglects the poor and does not acknowledge God. The wise person (or righteous person) is consistently portrayed as someone who thinks ahead, prioritizes the right things, understands that God's plans are always best, and seeks to honor God.

We have heard Solomon make statements like this before, right? Sometimes we think our own wisdom will lead us to our best lives. Sometimes we rely on things, people, or even ourselves to "outwise" God. This is what Solomon warns us against. Our wisdom never exceeds God's wisdom. We can count on our wisdom failing us, but God's wisdom always makes His plans succeed.

Ancient military leaders would compare the number of horses and chariots in their army to their enemy's horses and chariots to determine their chances of victory. In Proverbs 21:31, Solomon confirms that no matter how many resources we start with, God's plans always come out on top in the end. The Israelites won battles against much larger armies than theirs time and time again. Why? Because victory rests with the

Lord! A classic example of this is David's victory against Goliath (1 Samuel 17). God's plans always win because His wisdom knows best.

The Bottom Line

God's plans always succeed.

EXPERIENCE

Reread Proverbs 21:30-31. Rewrite these verses in your own words, as if you were writing them for one of your friends or a sibling.

What is one foolish thing you've been doing or foolish plan you've made that you can avoid in the coming weeks, months, or years?

What would be a wise alternative to that foolish activity or plan? How can you pursue this wise alternative in the coming weeks, months, or years?

Takeaway and Pray

My takeaway from this experience is

My prayer today is a

__ REQUEST __ CONFESSION __ PRAISE

boundary markers

Proverbs 22

Know before You Go

We are introduced to Solomon's "thirty precepts of the sages."

Read the Passage

¹ A sterling reputation is better than striking it rich;
  a gracious spirit is better than money in the bank.

² The rich and the poor shake hands as equals—
  GOD made them both!

³ A prudent person sees trouble coming and ducks;
  a simpleton walks in blindly and is clobbered.

⁴ The payoff for meekness and Fear-of-GOD
  is plenty and honor and a satisfying life.

⁵ The perverse travel a dangerous road, potholed and mud-slick;
      if you know what's good for you, stay clear of it.

⁶ Point your kids in the right direction—
      when they're old they won't be lost.

⁷ The poor are always ruled over by the rich,
      so don't borrow and put yourself under their power.

⁸ Whoever sows sin reaps weeds,
      and bullying anger sputters into nothing.

⁹ Generous hands are blessed hands
      because they give bread to the poor.

¹⁰ Kick out the troublemakers and things will quiet down;
      you need a break from bickering and griping!

¹¹ GOD loves the pure-hearted and well-spoken;
      good leaders also delight in their friendship.

¹² GOD guards knowledge with a passion,
      but he'll have nothing to do with deception.

¹³ The loafer says, "There's a lion on the loose!
      If I go out I'll be eaten alive!"

¹⁴ The mouth of a prostitute is a bottomless pit;
      you'll fall in that pit if you're on the outs with GOD.

¹⁵ Young people are prone to foolishness and fads;
      the cure comes through tough-minded discipline.

[16] Exploit the poor or glad-hand the rich—whichever,
>   you'll end up the poorer for it.

[17-21] Listen carefully to my wisdom;
>   take to heart what I can teach you.
> You'll treasure its sweetness deep within;
>   you'll give it bold expression in your speech.
> To make sure your foundation is trust in GOD,
>   I'm laying it all out right now just for you.
> I'm giving you thirty sterling principles—
>   tested guidelines to live by.
> Believe me—these are truths that work,
>   and will keep you accountable
>   to those who sent you.

[22-23] Don't walk on the poor just because they're poor,
>   and don't use your position to crush the weak,
> Because GOD will come to their defense;
>   the life you took, he'll take from you and give back to them.

[24-25] Don't hang out with angry people;
>   don't keep company with hotheads.
> Bad temper is contagious—
>   don't get infected.

[26-27] Don't gamble on the pot of gold at the end of the rainbow,
>   pawning your house against a lucky chance.
> The time will come when you have to pay up;
>   you'll be left with nothing but the shirt on your back.

[28] Don't stealthily move back the boundary lines
>   staked out long ago by your ancestors.

²⁹ Observe people who are good at their work—
    skilled workers are always in demand and admired;
    they don't take a backseat to anyone.

After the Passage

Proverbs 22:1-16 follows the same format as Proverbs 10–21 with its two-phrase sentences. But Solomon changes the format halfway through the chapter when he introduces a new section. There are a few things to know about these "thirty sterling principles" (Proverbs 22:20):

- Each saying expands on a theme Solomon has already addressed earlier in the book.
- Each saying has its own theme.
- Each saying stresses the need for wisdom and knowledge.

Most of the sayings are pretty straightforward, but every once in a while Solomon uses language that we no longer understand. For instance, were you a bit confused by Proverbs 22:28? In ancient times, families used stones to mark off where their land started and stopped. Simply by moving a boundary stone you could change the size of your land, which in the ancient world changed your wealth and status. Solomon's advice, in modern language, is actually quite simple: We should not take what is not ours!

While we do not have boundary stones, there are many subtle ways we can take things that do not belong to us. Perhaps we lie about how many hours we've worked, don't split tips fairly, or fill up our water cups at restaurants with soda! Solomon's ancient language is a warning against those easy, subtle ways of taking what is not ours.

The Bottom Line

Don't take what is not yours.

EXPERIENCE

Over the next three days, create your own list of "sterling principles." Drawing on the advice you've already received from Solomon, create your own proverbs around these important areas of your life.

MY PROVERBS ABOUT HOW TO DEAL WITH TEMPTATION	MY PROVERBS ABOUT HOW TO RELATE TO MY PARENTS	MY PROVERBS ABOUT HOW TO TREAT OTHERS

Takeaway and Pray

My takeaway from this experience is

My prayer today is a

__ REQUEST   __ CONFESSION   __ PRAISE

to do or
not to do?

Proverbs 23

Know before You Go

Proverbs 23 is Solomon's master list of dos and don'ts for living a wise life.

Read the Passage

¹⁻³ When you go out to dinner with an influential person,
  mind your manners:
Don't gobble your food,
  don't talk with your mouth full.
And don't stuff yourself;
  bridle your appetite.

⁴⁻⁵ Don't wear yourself out trying to get rich;
  restrain yourself!
Riches disappear in the blink of an eye;
  wealth sprouts wings
  and flies off into the wild blue yonder.

⁶⁻⁸ Don't accept a meal from a tightwad;
> don't expect anything special.
He'll be as stingy with you as he is with himself;
> he'll say, "Eat! Drink!" but won't mean a word of it.
His miserly serving will turn your stomach
> when you realize the meal's a sham.

⁹ Don't bother talking sense to fools;
> they'll only poke fun at your words.

¹⁰⁻¹¹ Don't stealthily move back the boundary lines
> or cheat orphans out of their property,
For they have a powerful Advocate
> who will go to bat for them.

¹² Give yourselves to disciplined instruction;
> open your ears to tested knowledge.

¹³⁻¹⁴ Don't be afraid to correct your young ones;
> a spanking won't kill them.
A good spanking, in fact, might save them
> from something worse than death.

¹⁵⁻¹⁶ Dear child, if you become wise,
> I'll be one happy parent.
My heart will dance and sing
> to the tuneful truth you'll speak.

¹⁷⁻¹⁸ Don't for a minute envy careless rebels;
> soak yourself in the Fear-of-God—
That's where your future lies.
> *Then* you won't be left with an armload of nothing.

¹⁹⁻²¹ Oh listen, dear child—become wise;
  point your life in the right direction.
Don't drink too much wine and get drunk;
  don't eat too much food and get fat.
Drunks and gluttons will end up on skid row,
  in a stupor and dressed in rags.

²²⁻²⁵ Listen with respect to the father who raised you,
  and when your mother grows old, don't neglect her.
Buy truth—don't sell it for love or money;
  buy wisdom, buy education, buy insight.
Parents rejoice when their children turn out well;
  wise children become proud parents.
So make your father happy!
  Make your mother proud!

²⁶ Dear child, I want your full attention;
  please do what I show you.

²⁷⁻²⁸ A prostitute is a bottomless pit;
  a loose woman can get you in deep trouble fast.
She'll take you for all you've got;
  she's worse than a pack of thieves.

²⁹⁻³⁵ Who are the people who are always crying the blues?
  Who do you know who reeks of self-pity?
Who keeps getting beaten up for no reason at all?
  Whose eyes are bleary and bloodshot?
It's those who spend the night with a bottle,
  for whom drinking is serious business.
Don't judge wine by its label,
  or its bouquet, or its full-bodied flavor.

Judge it rather by the hangover it leaves you with—
  the splitting headache, the queasy stomach.
Do you really prefer seeing double,
  with your speech all slurred,
Reeling and seasick,
  drunk as a sailor?
"They hit me," you'll say, "but it didn't hurt;
  they beat on me, but I didn't feel a thing.
When I'm sober enough to manage it,
  bring me another drink!"

After the Passage

Proverbs 23 introduces thirteen more of Solomon's "sterling principles" (Proverbs 22:20), with each asking, *To do or not to do?* While most of Solomon's sayings in Proverbs 23 are full of common sense, life can often distract us from choosing well, even if we know better. Committing in advance "to do or not to do" can help us when the "obvious" choice seems confusing.

You may have noticed an interesting theme in the first few sayings in this chapter. Solomon cautions people about their interactions with the influential (Proverbs 23:1-3) and warns us against trying to get rich (Proverbs 23:4-5). He also cautions against people who act generous but in their hearts are only concerned with money (Proverbs 23:6-8). All this advice points to a common theme throughout the book of Proverbs: There is more to life than accumulating wealth.

Although Proverbs 23:13-14 is often unpopular with kids, it contains great advice! Solomon, himself a father trying to train his son, explains that parental discipline is actually an act of wisdom. Appropriate discipline, although surely not fun to receive, can help train and protect us. Proper discipline helps steer us away from unwise actions and protect us from the dangerous consequences of foolish choices. Think about this the next time you face consequences for your actions, and perhaps it will change your attitude, even if just a bit.

The Bottom Line

Committing in advance to a set of dos and don'ts can help you make wise decisions in important moments.

EXPERIENCE

Continue to create your own list of "sterling principles." Drawing on the advice you've already received from Solomon, create your own proverbs around these important areas of your life.

MY PROVERBS ABOUT RELATIONSHIPS	MY PROVERBS ABOUT FAMILY	MY PROVERBS ABOUT MONEY

Takeaway and Pray

My takeaway from this experience is

My prayer today is a

__ REQUEST __ CONFESSION __ PRAISE

it takes wisdom to build a house

Proverbs 24

Know before You Go

We reach the end of Solomon's thirty precepts of the sages, and he compares wisdom to building a house.

Read the Passage

1-2 Don't envy bad people;
    don't even want to be around them.
All they think about is causing a disturbance;
    all they talk about is making trouble.

3-4 It takes wisdom to build a house,
    and understanding to set it on a firm foundation;
It takes knowledge to furnish its rooms
    with fine furniture and beautiful draperies.

5-6 It's better to be wise than strong;
    intelligence outranks muscle any day.

Strategic planning is the key to warfare;
    to win, you need a lot of good counsel.

[7] Wise conversation is way over the head of fools;
    in a serious discussion they haven't a clue.

[8-9] The person who's always cooking up some evil
      soon gets a reputation as prince of rogues.
Fools incubate sin;
    cynics desecrate beauty.

[10] If you fall to pieces in a crisis,
    there wasn't much to you in the first place.

[11-12] Rescue the perishing;
      don't hesitate to step in and help.
If you say, "Hey, that's none of my business,"
    will that get you off the hook?
Someone is watching you closely, you know—
    Someone not impressed with weak excuses.

[13-14] Eat honey, dear child—it's good for you—
      and delicacies that melt in your mouth.
Likewise knowledge,
    and wisdom for your soul—
Get that and your future's secured,
    your hope is on solid rock.

[15-16] Don't interfere with good people's lives;
      don't try to get the best of them.
No matter how many times you trip them up,
    God-loyal people don't stay down long;

Soon they're up on their feet,
    while the wicked end up flat on their faces.

17-18 Don't laugh when your enemy falls;
    don't gloat over his collapse.
God might see, and become very provoked,
    and then take pity on his plight.

19-20 Don't bother your head with braggarts
    or wish you could succeed like the wicked.
Those people have no future at all;
    they're headed down a dead-end street.

21-22 Fear God, dear child—respect your leaders;
    don't be defiant or mutinous.
Without warning your life can turn upside down,
    and who knows how or when it might happen?

23 It's wrong, very wrong,
    to go along with injustice.

24-25 Whoever whitewashes the wicked
    gets a black mark in the history books,
But whoever exposes the wicked
    will be thanked and rewarded.

26 An honest answer
    is like a warm hug.

27 First plant your fields;
    then build your barn.

²⁸⁻²⁹ Don't talk about your neighbors behind their backs—
     no slander or gossip, please.
   Don't say to anyone, "I'll get back at you for what you did to me.
     I'll make you pay for what you did!"

³⁰⁻³⁴ One day I walked by the field of an old lazybones,
     and then passed the vineyard of a slob;
   They were overgrown with weeds,
     thick with thistles, all the fences broken down.
   I took a long look and pondered what I saw;
     the fields preached me a sermon and I listened:
   "A nap here, a nap there, a day off here, a day off there,
     sit back, take it easy—do you know what comes next?
   Just this: You can look forward to a dirt-poor life,
     with poverty as your permanent houseguest!"

After the Passage

Wisdom is a lot like building a house. A solid, sturdy house is a huge commitment. It takes lots of time, tons of planning, plenty of money to buy all the supplies, and a team of experienced professionals to put it all together. It takes intentionality to do it right the first time (Proverbs 24:3-4).

Solomon adds another detail to the picture in Proverbs 24:27. He offers advice on the sequence of homebuilding: Before building the structure, first get the fields ready. Before you build *on* the land, *prepare* the land. The outdoor work comes before the indoor work.

In Solomon's day, the fields were often a family's main source of income in the form of crops, produce, and grain. This food would end up at their table and would feed their animals. The family would also sell or trade the crops to buy what they needed. The fields were crucial for survival.

So taking care of the fields was a more urgent task than setting up the house. Just think—if there were no crops to sell, there would be no way to buy supplies to build the house.

Proverbs 24:27 is a great reminder of how we ought to prioritize our tasks. Often we want to rush right to the end goal (the house). Solomon encourages us to zoom out and do all the prep work needed in order to make the final project a success. The wise look at the entire project!

The Bottom Line

The wise person looks at the big picture and sets priorities to ensure success.

EXPERIENCE

Continue to create your own list of "sterling principles." Drawing on the advice you've already received from Solomon, create your own proverbs around these important areas of your life.

MY PROVERBS ABOUT WORK	MY PROVERBS ABOUT HEALTH

MY PROVERBS ABOUT FRIENDS	MY PROVERBS ABOUT HONORING GOD

Takeaway and Pray

My takeaway from this experience is

My prayer today is a

__ REQUEST __ CONFESSION __ PRAISE

kings, companions, and enemies

Proverbs 25

Know before You Go

We begin a new section: wise sayings of Solomon collected by King Hezekiah's scribes.

Read the Passage

¹ There are also these proverbs of Solomon,
   collected by scribes of Hezekiah, king of Judah.

² God delights in concealing things;
   scientists delight in discovering things.

³ Like the horizons for breadth and the ocean for depth,
   the understanding of a good leader is broad and deep.

⁴⁻⁵ Remove impurities from the silver
   and the silversmith can craft a fine chalice;
Remove the wicked from leadership
   and authority will be credible and God-honoring.

⁶⁻⁷ Don't work yourself into the spotlight;
  don't push your way into the place of prominence.
 It's better to be promoted to a place of honor
  than face humiliation by being demoted.

⁸ Don't jump to conclusions—there may be
  a perfectly good explanation for what you just saw.

⁹⁻¹⁰ In the heat of an argument,
  don't betray confidences;
 Word is sure to get around,
  and no one will trust you.

¹¹⁻¹² The right word at the right time
  is like a custom-made piece of jewelry,
 And a wise friend's timely reprimand
  is like a gold ring slipped on your finger.

¹³ Reliable friends who do what they say
  are like cool drinks in sweltering heat—refreshing!

¹⁴ Like billowing clouds that bring no rain
  is the person who talks big but never produces.

¹⁵ Patient persistence pierces through indifference;
  gentle speech breaks down rigid defenses.

¹⁶⁻¹⁷ When you're given a box of candy, don't gulp it all down;
  eat too much chocolate and you'll make yourself sick;
 And when you find a friend, don't outwear your welcome;
  show up at all hours and he'll soon get fed up.

¹⁸ Anyone who tells lies against the neighbors
    in court or on the street is a loose cannon.

¹⁹ Trusting a double-crosser when you're in trouble
    is like biting down on an abscessed tooth.

²⁰ Singing light songs to the heavyhearted
    is like pouring salt in their wounds.

²¹⁻²² If you see your enemy hungry, go buy him lunch;
    if he's thirsty, bring him a drink.
  Your generosity will surprise him with goodness,
    and God will look after you.

²³ A north wind brings stormy weather,
    and a gossipy tongue stormy looks.

²⁴ Better to live alone in a tumbledown shack
    than share a mansion with a nagging spouse.

²⁵ Like a cool drink of water when you're worn out and weary
    is a letter from a long-lost friend.

²⁶ A good person who gives in to a bad person
    is a muddied spring, a polluted well.

²⁷ It's not smart to stuff yourself with sweets,
    nor is glory piled on glory good for you.

²⁸ A person without self-control
    is like a house with its doors and windows knocked out.

After the Passage

Proverbs 25:1 drops a few new people. Here's what we know: King Hezekiah, who ruled long after King Solomon, ordered his scribes to collect Solomon's lost writings. While not named, these scribes might have been people like the prophets Isaiah, Hosea, and Micah. These sayings focus on how we should interact with leaders, companions, and enemies.

The leader referenced in Proverbs 25 is either our heavenly King (God) or earthly leaders (like Kings Solomon and Hezekiah). In our interactions with leaders, it is important to be humble. Trying to make ourselves seem impressive only backfires, especially if we do so by stepping on others. Proverbs 25:6-7 paints a picture of the leader embarrassing those who try to impress him, as opposed to those who serve humbly. The wise person practices trustworthiness (Proverbs 25:9-10). Reliable friends refresh the spirits of others (Proverbs 25:13).

In Proverbs 25:8-10, the focus shifts away from the leader. The people in view here might be referred to as our companions—family, friends, neighbors, people we know well. Solomon warns us to be careful about how we handle arguments and conflicts. Making enemies of our companions is not wise. It often leads to embarrassment, sadness, and sometimes even the loss of friends. If we do not treat our companions well, people will have a hard time trusting us.

"Enemies" are the people we do not get along with. Enemies are just a part of life. Solomon shows us how to treat such people in Proverbs 25:21-22: We are to help them when they need it, even when they do not ask. Whether people are hungry or thirsty, need someone to listen to them, need a ride to school, or need help studying for a test, wise people offer compassion—even to people they do not agree with. When we do this, God does not miss it. He notices and rewards us.

True kindness is the greatest weapon we have; in fact, this exact passage is referenced in Romans 12:20, when the apostle Paul is addressing how God's people should treat their enemies. If you really want to drive your enemies crazy, be kind to them!

The Bottom Line

We are to be humble before kings, kind to companions, and caring to enemies.

EXPERIENCE

Who are the kings (authority figures), companions (friends/family), and enemies (people you disagree with or don't get along with) in your life?

KINGS	COMPANIONS	ENEMIES
How can you be humble with them?	How can you be kind to them?	How can you care for them?

Takeaway and Pray

My takeaway from this experience is

My prayer today is a

___ REQUEST ___ CONFESSION ___ PRAISE

contradictions?

Proverbs 26

Know before You Go

The sayings collected by
Hezekiah's scribes continue as
we circle back to the doom
that awaits fools.

Read the Passage

¹ We no more give honors to fools
than pray for snow in summer or rain during harvest.

² You have as little to fear from an undeserved curse
as from the dart of a wren or the swoop of a swallow.

³ A whip for the racehorse, a tiller for the sailboat—
and a stick for the back of fools!

⁴ Don't respond to the stupidity of a fool;
you'll only look foolish yourself.

⁵ Answer a fool in simple terms
    so he doesn't get a swelled head.

⁶ You're only asking for trouble
    when you send a message by a fool.

⁷ A proverb quoted by fools
    is limp as a wet noodle.

⁸ Putting a fool in a place of honor
    is like setting a mud brick on a marble column.

⁹ To ask a moron to quote a proverb
    is like putting a scalpel in the hands of a drunk.

¹⁰ Hire a fool or a drunk
    and you shoot yourself in the foot.

¹¹ As a dog eats its own vomit,
    so fools recycle silliness.

¹² See that man who thinks he's so smart?
    You can expect far more from a fool than from him.

¹³ Loafers say, "It's dangerous out there!
    Tigers are prowling the streets!"
    and then pull the covers back over their heads.

¹⁴ Just as a door turns on its hinges,
    so a lazybones turns back over in bed.

¹⁵ A shiftless sluggard puts his fork in the pie,
    but is too lazy to lift it to his mouth.

¹⁶ Dreamers fantasize their self-importance;
    they think they are smarter
    than a whole college faculty.

¹⁷ You grab a mad dog by the ears
    when you butt into a quarrel that's none of your business.

¹⁸⁻¹⁹ People who shrug off deliberate deceptions,
    saying, "I didn't mean it, I was only joking,"
Are worse than careless campers
    who walk away from smoldering campfires.

²⁰ When you run out of wood, the fire goes out;
    when the gossip ends, the quarrel dies down.

²¹ A quarrelsome person in a dispute
    is like kerosene thrown on a fire.

²² Listening to gossip is like eating cheap candy;
    do you want junk like that in your belly?

²³ Smooth talk from an evil heart
    is like glaze on cracked pottery.

²⁴⁻²⁶ Your enemy shakes hands and greets you like an old friend,
    all the while plotting against you.
When he speaks warmly to you, don't believe him for a minute;
    he's just waiting for the chance to rip you off.

No matter how shrewdly he conceals his malice,
eventually his evil will be exposed in public.

²⁷ Malice backfires;
spite boomerangs.

²⁸ Liars hate their victims;
flatterers sabotage trust.

After the Passage

Proverbs 26 contains a classic example of what many believe to be a contradiction in the Bible. A *contradiction* is a pair of statements that say the opposite of each other. Contradiction is especially problematic for the Bible because we believe the Bible is the Word of God, and if statements in the Bible tell you to do opposite things, how do you know which statement is God's true word to us? For that matter, if we decide that one statement in the Bible being true means that another statement in the Bible is not true, how can we trust the rest of Scripture?

The statements we are talking about are in Proverbs 26:4-5. In verse 4, Solomon tells us not to respond to a fool. In verse 5, however, Solomon says to answer a fool. So which is it?

Rather than being a contradiction, Proverbs 26:4-5 is actually a classic example of how the book of Proverbs works! Proverbs offers us God's wisdom in principles that are generally true and descriptions of how the world usually works (or should work). For instance, Proverbs 10:4 teaches that lazy people have a hard time gaining wealth. Is this true in most cases? Yes! But are there exceptions—times when lazy people acquire great wealth? Also yes! Proverbs are meant to guide us in how the world generally works.

Proverbs 26:4-5 is a great example of why we need wisdom: Deciding which approach to take when answering a fool requires discernment. According to verse 5, there are times when correcting a fool will actually help them become more wise! In those cases, when a fool is open to feedback and correction, you should help them see their mistakes.

And yet according to verse 4, there will be people in your life who have no desire to hear the truth. Instead of embracing your wise feedback, they will just argue with you. The longer you argue with them, the more foolish you become!

So then, both verse 4 and verse 5 can be true—depending on your circumstance!

The Bottom Line

Applying the wisdom of Proverbs requires us to practice wisdom.

EXPERIENCE

Think of one or two proverbs you've read so far that are generally but (seemingly) not always true. Write them below.

Who is someone in your life you consistently try to correct but usually end up in an argument with?

Takeaway and Pray

My takeaway from this experience is

My prayer today is a

__ REQUEST __ CONFESSION __ PRAISE

WHEN YOU ARGUE
WITH SOMEONE BEING
FOOLISH, ASK GOD TO
GIVE YOU PATIENCE AND
DISCERNMENT SO YOU
DON'T ENGAGE THEM
IN A FOOLISH WAY.

no Negative Nellies please!

Proverbs 27

Know before You Go

Quarrelsome people drain you, while wise people sharpen you.

Read the Passage

¹ Don't brashly announce what you're going to do tomorrow;
    you don't know the first thing about tomorrow.

² Don't call attention to yourself;
    let others do that for you.

³ Carrying a log across your shoulders
    while you're hefting a boulder with your arms
Is nothing compared to the burden
    of putting up with a fool.

⁴ We're blasted by anger and swamped by rage,
    but who can survive jealousy?

⁵ A spoken reprimand is better
    than approval that's never expressed.

⁶ The wounds from a lover are worth it;
    kisses from an enemy do you in.

⁷ When you've stuffed yourself, you refuse dessert;
    when you're starved, you could eat a horse.

⁸ People who won't settle down, wandering hither and yon,
    are like restless birds, flitting to and fro.

⁹ Just as lotions and fragrance give sensual delight,
    a sweet friendship refreshes the soul.

¹⁰ Don't leave your friends or your parents' friends
    and run home to your family when things get rough;
Better a nearby friend
    than a distant family.

¹¹ Become wise, dear child, and make me happy;
    then nothing the world throws my way will upset me.

¹² A prudent person sees trouble coming and ducks;
    a simpleton walks in blindly and is clobbered.

¹³ Hold tight to collateral on any loan to a stranger;
    be wary of accepting what a transient has pawned.

¹⁴ If you wake your friend in the early morning
    by shouting "Rise and shine!"

It will sound to him
    more like a curse than a blessing.

15-16 A nagging spouse is like
    the drip, drip, drip of a leaky faucet;
You can't turn it off,
    and you can't get away from it.

17 You use steel to sharpen steel,
    and one friend sharpens another.

18 If you care for your orchard, you'll enjoy its fruit;
    if you honor your boss, you'll be honored.

19 Just as water mirrors your face,
    so your face mirrors your heart.

20 Hell has a voracious appetite,
    and lust just never quits.

21 The purity of silver and gold is tested
    by putting them in the fire;
The purity of human hearts is tested
    by giving them a little fame.

22 Pound on a fool all you like—
    you can't pound out foolishness.

23-27 Know your sheep by name;
    carefully attend to your flocks;
(Don't take them for granted;
    possessions don't last forever, you know.)

And then, when the crops are in
    and the harvest is stored in the barns,
You can knit sweaters from lambs' wool,
    and sell your goats for a profit;
There will be plenty of milk and meat
    to last your family through the winter.

After the Passage

In all our praise of King Solomon's wisdom, we have neglected to mention his primary weakness: women. Read 1 Kings 11:1-10. King Solomon had seven hundred wives (not to mention three hundred concubines), which—apart from not being wise—was actually against God's law. Many of Solomon's wives followed other gods from other nations. They helped turn him away from the one true God.

Proverbs 27:15-16 describes life with an unpleasant spouse, but this is not just dating advice or counsel against marrying a difficult person. It is a warning about the impact negative people can have on our lives. A difficult person can take down the person they are in a relationship with.

This passage speaks of a spouse, but it could just as easily refer to a friend, teammate, or enemy. Living with a difficult, angry person, according to Proverbs 27:15-16, is like having a leak that continues to drip and drip. They cause problems that just won't go away!

Contrast this picture with the very next verse (Proverbs 27:17). While people can be annoyances, they can also sharpen you and make you better. Our relationships, especially our close relationships, can have a tremendous impact on our lives. They can bring joy, offer strength, and make us better, or they can be frustrating, time-consuming, and aggravating. And while you can't always choose whom you spend time with, you can choose your closest friends—and your spouse!

When making decisions about which relationships you want to prioritize, avoid quarrelsome people and choose people who will sharpen you.

The Bottom Line

Quarrelsome people drain you. Wise people sharpen you.

EXPERIENCE

Think through the differences between quarrelsome people and sharpening people described in Proverbs 27.

Is there anyone in your life who is like the drip of a leaky faucet, constantly causing issues in your life? How can you minimize their impact on your life?

Are there people in your life who would consider you the leaky faucet? How can you make their lives less difficult?

Who in your life sharpens you? How do they make you better? How can you thank them for the ways they make you better?

Who are some friends you can help sharpen? How can you do this? What would they say if you asked them?

Takeaway and Pray

My takeaway from this experience is

My prayer today is a

__ REQUEST __ CONFESSION __ PRAISE

slow and steady wins the race

Proverbs 28

Know before You Go

Proverbs 28 describes rushing toward personal success versus walking with integrity before the Lord.

Read the Passage

¹ The wicked are edgy with guilt, ready to run off
   even when no one's after them;
Honest people are relaxed and confident,
   bold as lions.

² When the country is in chaos,
   everybody has a plan to fix it—
But it takes a leader of real understanding
   to straighten things out.

³ The wicked who oppress the poor
   are like a hailstorm that beats down the harvest.

⁴ If you desert God's law, you're free to embrace depravity;
    if you love God's law, you fight for it tooth and nail.

⁵ Justice makes no sense to the evilminded;
    those who seek GOD know it inside and out.

⁶ It's better to be poor and direct
    than rich and crooked.

⁷ Practice God's law—get a reputation for wisdom;
    hang out with a loose crowd—embarrass your family.

⁸ Get as rich as you want
    through cheating and extortion,
But eventually some friend of the poor
    is going to give it all back to them.

⁹ God has no use for the prayers
    of the people who won't listen to him.

¹⁰ Lead good people down a wrong path
    and you'll come to a bad end;
    do good and you'll be rewarded for it.

¹¹ The rich think they know it all,
    but the poor can see right through them.

¹² When good people are promoted, everything is great,
    but when the bad are in charge, watch out!

¹³ You can't whitewash your sins and get by with it;
    you find mercy by admitting and leaving them.

[14] A tenderhearted person lives a blessed life;
  a hardhearted person lives a hard life.

[15] Lions roar and bears charge—
  and the wicked lord it over the poor.

[16] Among leaders who lack insight, abuse abounds,
  but for one who hates corruption, the future is bright.

[17] A murderer haunted by guilt
  is doomed—there's no helping him.

[18] Walk straight—live well and be saved;
  a devious life is a doomed life.

[19] Work your garden—you'll end up with plenty of food;
  play and party—you'll end up with an empty plate.

[20] Committed and persistent work pays off;
  get-rich-quick schemes are ripoffs.

[21] Playing favorites is always a bad thing;
  you can do great harm in seemingly harmless ways.

[22] A miser in a hurry to get rich
  doesn't know that he'll end up broke.

[23] In the end, serious reprimand is appreciated
  far more than bootlicking flattery.

²⁴ Anyone who robs father and mother
    and says, "So, what's wrong with that?"
    is worse than a pirate.

²⁵ A grasping person stirs up trouble,
    but trust in GOD brings a sense of well-being.

²⁶ If you think you know it all, you're a fool for sure;
    real survivors learn wisdom from others.

²⁷ Be generous to the poor—you'll never go hungry;
    shut your eyes to their needs, and run a gauntlet of curses.

²⁸ When corruption takes over, good people go underground,
    but when the crooks are thrown out, it's safe to come out.

After the Passage

You've probably seen shows or movies that portray power-hungry villains who rush in seeking quick success, easy money, and unrivaled power only to fail miserably in the end. While it is easy to pick out such foolish people on a screen, it is a little harder to recognize them among the people around us.

In Proverbs 28, Solomon contrasts the strife and greed of a fool with the integrity of a wise person. He describes how this shows up both in how people lead others and in the way we live our lives as regular people.

People who seek quick personal gain usually lack self-control. But if controlling greed is difficult for an average person, imagine how difficult it would be for a person with power! A powerful person who acts wickedly is like a charging bear or roaring lion (Proverbs 28:15). Destruction follows. Wealthy people—even if they choose not to walk on the path of integrity—often think what they are doing is right (Proverbs 28:11). Hardheartedness gets people into trouble (Proverbs 28:14). By rushing in and taking shortcuts, foolish people make bad decisions. They rarely ever gain the power or success they desire—and when they start with power or success, they cause more harm than good (Proverbs 28:12, 20, 22).

Solomon saves a few words for wise people in Proverbs 28. They are "bold as lions" (Proverbs 28:1). They bring stability (Proverbs 28:2) and justice (Proverbs 28:5). They don't rush after personal success or take shortcuts. They don't define success as power, control, or riches. For a wise person, walking steadily in integrity toward God each day is true success. A wise person's true treasure is the Lord (Proverbs 28:25).

The Bottom Line

The foolish person rushes after personal gain; the wise person walks steadily with the Lord.

EXPERIENCE

Write out Proverbs 28:20 and Proverbs 28:22 in the space below. Try to memorize them over the course of the next week.

Write the same verses somewhere you'll see them regularly. Let them be a reminder to resist the temptation to pursue wealth instead of pursuing God.

Takeaway and Pray

My takeaway from this experience is

My prayer today is a

__ REQUEST __ CONFESSION __ PRAISE

o captain, my captain!

Proverbs 29

Know before You Go

Solomon's final proverb describes a battle between a gang of cynics and a group of sages.

Read the Passage

¹ For people who hate discipline
    and only get more stubborn,
There'll come a day when life tumbles in and they break,
    but by then it'll be too late to help them.

² When good people run things, everyone is glad,
    but when the ruler is bad, everyone groans.

³ If you love wisdom, you'll delight your parents,
    but you'll destroy their trust if you run with prostitutes.

[4] A leader of good judgment gives stability;
    an exploiting leader leaves a trail of waste.

[5] A flattering neighbor is up to no good;
    he's probably planning to take advantage of you.

[6] Evil people fall into their own traps;
    good people run the other way, glad to escape.

[7] The good-hearted understand what it's like to be poor;
    the hardhearted haven't the faintest idea.

[8] A gang of cynics can upset a whole city;
    a group of sages can calm everyone down.

[9] A sage trying to work things out with a fool
    gets only scorn and sarcasm for his trouble.

[10] Murderers hate honest people;
    moral folks encourage them.

[11] A fool lets it all hang out;
    a sage quietly mulls it over.

[12] When a leader listens to malicious gossip,
    all the workers get infected with evil.

[13] The poor and their abusers have at least something in common:
    they can both *see*—their sight, GOD's gift!

[14] Leadership gains authority and respect
    when the voiceless poor are treated fairly.

¹⁵ Wise discipline imparts wisdom;
    spoiled adolescents embarrass their parents.

¹⁶ When degenerates take charge, crime runs wild,
    but the righteous will eventually observe their collapse.

¹⁷ Discipline your children; you'll be glad you did—
    they'll turn out delightful to live with.

¹⁸ If people can't see what God is doing,
    they stumble all over themselves;
  But when they attend to what he reveals,
    they are most blessed.

¹⁹ It takes more than talk to keep workers in line;
    mere words go in one ear and out the other.

²⁰ Observe the people who always talk before they think—
    even simpletons are better off than they are.

²¹ If you let people treat you like a doormat,
    you'll be quite forgotten in the end.

²² Angry people stir up a lot of discord;
    the intemperate stir up trouble.

²³ Pride lands you flat on your face;
    humility prepares you for honors.

²⁴ Befriend an outlaw
    and become an enemy to yourself.

When the victims cry out,
    you'll be included in their curses
    if you're a coward to their cause in court.

[25] The fear of human opinion disables;
    trusting in GOD protects you from that.

[26] Everyone tries to get help from the leader,
    but only GOD will give us justice.

[27] Good people can't stand the sight of deliberate evil;
    the wicked can't stand the sight of well-chosen goodness.

After the Passage

We have seen tension building as we have come to know the character of both wisdom and folly. They are indeed mortal enemies with very little in common. In his final collection of proverbs, Solomon demonstrates that these two approaches to life ultimately can't coexist. Proverbs 29:10 uses the most violent language in the chapter, referencing hate and murder. Throughout Proverbs 29, however, we see that fools have strong feelings toward the wise. They are prepared to do whatever it takes to get rid of them. In battle terms, they are prepared for casualties and are not taking any prisoners.

The chart below describes the character of an army of folly. The wise, by contrast, are motivated by justice and are prepared to defend integrity, protect righteousness, and maintain stability. They, too, are prepared for whatever it takes.

PROVERBS 29	A GANG OF CYNICS
Proverbs 29:10	They hate people of integrity.
Proverbs 29:11	They are undisciplined.
Proverbs 29:16	They live in wickedness and create chaos.
Proverbs 29:18	They refuse to learn self-control.
Proverbs 29:20	They speak without thinking.
Proverbs 29:22	They stir up conflict among themselves.
Proverbs 29:23	They are entitled, arrogant, and prideful.

Solomon's final word in Proverbs 29:27 is a perfect summary of a fundamental contrast in Proverbs: The good detest evil, and the evil detest good.

The Bottom Line

Wisdom and folly battle each other, but wisdom will win the war.

EXPERIENCE

From your own life experience, create a list of contrasting characteristics between foolishness/wickedness and wisdom/righteousness.

The fool _____ , but the wise _____ .

The fool _____ , but the wise _____ .

The fool _____ , but the wise _____ .

The fool _____ , but the wise _____ .

What is one foolish thing in your life you can eliminate and replace with wisdom?

Takeaway and Pray

My takeaway from this experience is

My prayer today is a

__ **REQUEST** __ **CONFESSION** __ **PRAISE**

three—no, four things

Proverbs 30

Know before You Go

We are introduced to a new person, Agur, and his inspired sayings of wisdom.

Read the Passage

¹⁻² The skeptic swore, "There is no God!
No God!—I can do anything I want!
I'm more animal than human;
so-called human intelligence escapes me.

³⁻⁴ "I flunked 'wisdom.'
I see no evidence of a holy God.
Has anyone ever seen Anyone
climb into Heaven and take charge?
grab the winds and control them?
gather the rains in his bucket?
stake out the ends of the earth?

Just tell me his name, tell me the names of his sons.
    Come on now—tell me!"

5-6 The believer replied, "Every promise of God proves true;
    he protects everyone who runs to him for help.
So don't second-guess him;
    he might take you to task and show up your lies."

7-9 And then he prayed, "God, I'm asking for two things
    before I die; don't refuse me—
Banish lies from my lips
    and liars from my presence.
Give me enough food to live on,
    neither too much nor too little.
If I'm too full, I might get independent,
    saying, 'God? Who needs him?'
If I'm poor, I might steal
    and dishonor the name of my God."

10 Don't blow the whistle on your fellow workers
    behind their backs;
They'll accuse you of being underhanded,
    and then *you'll* be the guilty one!

11 Don't curse your father
    or fail to bless your mother.

12 Don't imagine yourself to be quite presentable
    when you haven't had a bath in weeks.

¹³ Don't be stuck-up
    and think you're better than everyone else.

¹⁴ Don't be greedy,
    merciless and cruel as wolves,
Tearing into the poor and feasting on them,
    shredding the needy to pieces only to discard them.

¹⁵⁻¹⁶ A freeloader has twin daughters
    named "Gimme" and "Gimme more."

Three things are never satisfied,
    no, there are four that never say, "That's enough, thank you!"—

hell,
a barren womb,
a parched land,
a forest fire.

¹⁷ An eye that disdains a father
    and despises a mother—
that eye will be plucked out by wild vultures
    and consumed by young eagles.

¹⁸⁻¹⁹ Three things amaze me,
    no, four things I'll never understand—

how an eagle flies so high in the sky,
how a snake glides over a rock,
how a ship navigates the ocean,
why adolescents act the way they do.

²⁰ Here's how a prostitute operates:
    she has sex with her client,
Takes a bath,
    then asks, "Who's next?"

²¹⁻²³ Three things are too much for even the earth to bear,
    yes, four things shake its foundations—

    when the janitor becomes the boss,
    when a fool gets rich,
    when a prostitute is voted "woman of the year,"
    when a "girlfriend" replaces a faithful wife.

²⁴⁻²⁸ There are four small creatures,
    wisest of the wise they are—

    ants—frail as they are,
       get plenty of food in for the winter;
    marmots—vulnerable as they are,
       manage to arrange for rock-solid homes;
    locusts—leaderless insects,
       yet they strip the field like an army regiment;
    lizards—easy enough to catch,
       but they sneak past vigilant palace guards.

²⁹⁻³¹ There are three solemn dignitaries,
    four that are impressive in their bearing—

a lion, king of the beasts, deferring to none;

a rooster, proud and strutting;

a billy goat;

a head of state in stately procession.

32-33 If you're dumb enough to call attention to yourself

by offending people and making rude gestures,

Don't be surprised if someone bloodies your nose.

Churned milk turns into butter;

riled emotions turn into fist fights.

After the Passage

You can consider the words of Agur to be like the extended edition of Proverbs. Hezekiah's wise men, whom we talked about in the reading on Proverbs 25, included these in the collection of Proverbs. They felt that Agur's sayings were wise and important enough to stand next to Solomon's wisdom. While Agur's sayings are wise, he wrote very differently from Solomon. He liked using lists and putting his wisdom into separate categories. Let's look at the groups of sayings that Agur describes in Proverbs 30:

- four things that are never satisfied (Proverbs 30:15-16)
- four things that are hard to understand (Proverbs 30:18-19)
- four things that cause the earth to tremble (Proverbs 30:21-23)
- four things that are small and wise (Proverbs 30:24-28)
- four things that are solemn and impressive (Proverbs 30:29-31)

Agur took the time to notice and think about each of these things carefully as God revealed them to him. Think about it yourself: The bigger a fire gets, the more it destroys—it is never satisfied. An eagle soaring in the air without falling or crashing is amazing to watch. Think about how wrong it feels when a fool has an easy life without working for it. Looking for God's wisdom in the everyday things of each day helps us see Him around us all the time. Or, to put it another way, all wisdom is God's wisdom.

When we notice the incredible way the world works, we are actually noticing the wisdom of God, who created everything we see. When we start to realize how all-encompassing God's wisdom is, we cannot help but love Him more.

The Bottom Line

The wisdom of God is revealed to us in everyday life.

EXPERIENCE

One of the many lessons from Proverbs 30 is that the wisdom of God is all around us all the time! Take some time over the next few days to look for the wisdom of God in these everyday categories. When you notice something, write it down here, and then take time to praise God for His wisdom.

WISDOM FROM EVERYDAY NATURE (ANIMALS, PLANTS)	WISDOM FROM EVERYDAY TASKS (CHORES, SCHOOLWORK)
WISDOM FROM EVERYDAY RELATIONSHIPS (FRIENDS, FAMILY)	WISDOM FROM EVERYDAY CULTURE (SHOWS, MUSIC, MOVIES, SOCIAL MEDIA)

Takeaway and Pray

My takeaway from this experience is

My prayer today is a

__ REQUEST __ CONFESSION __ PRAISE

what a woman!

Proverbs 31

Know before You Go

The last chapter of Proverbs describes the responsibility of kings and the noble character of a good wife.

Read the Passage

¹ The words of King Lemuel,
    the strong advice his mother gave him:

²⁻³ "Oh, son of mine, what can you be thinking of!
    Child whom I bore! The son I dedicated to God!
Don't dilute your strength on fortune-hunting women,
    promiscuous women who shipwreck leaders.

⁴⁻⁷ "Leaders can't afford to make fools of themselves,
    gulping wine and swilling beer,
Lest, hung over, they don't know right from wrong,
    and the people who depend on them are hurt.

Use wine and beer only as sedatives,
> to kill the pain and dull the ache
Of the terminally ill,
> for whom life is a living death.

8-9 "Speak up for the people who have no voice,
> for the rights of all the misfits.
Speak out for justice!
> Stand up for the poor and destitute!"

10-31 A good woman is hard to find,
> and worth far more than diamonds.
Her husband trusts her without reserve,
> and never has reason to regret it.
Never spiteful, she treats him generously
> all her life long.
She shops around for the best yarns and cottons,
> and enjoys knitting and sewing.
She's like a trading ship that sails to faraway places
> and brings back exotic surprises.
She's up before dawn, preparing breakfast
> for her family and organizing her day.
She looks over a field and buys it,
> then, with money she's put aside, plants a garden.
First thing in the morning, she dresses for work,
> rolls up her sleeves, eager to get started.
She senses the worth of her work,
> is in no hurry to call it quits for the day.
She's skilled in the crafts of home and hearth,
> diligent in homemaking.
She's quick to assist anyone in need,
> reaches out to help the poor.

She doesn't worry about her family when it snows;
    their winter clothes are all mended and ready to wear.
She makes her own clothing,
    and dresses in colorful linens and silks.
Her husband is greatly respected
    when he deliberates with the city fathers.
She designs gowns and sells them,
    brings the sweaters she knits to the dress shops.
Her clothes are well-made and elegant,
    and she always faces tomorrow with a smile.
When she speaks she has something worthwhile to say,
    and she always says it kindly.
She keeps an eye on everyone in her household,
    and keeps them all busy and productive.
Her children respect and bless her;
    her husband joins in with words of praise:
"Many women have done wonderful things,
    but you've outclassed them all!"
Charm can mislead and beauty soon fades.
    The woman to be admired and praised
    is the woman who lives in the Fear-of-God.
Give her everything she deserves!
    Adorn her life with praises!

After the Passage

Just as we were introduced to wisdom as a woman calling out in the streets in Proverbs 1, we now see another wise woman concluding Proverbs. The perfect book-end in discussing wisdom, the woman this time is the queen mother of King Lemuel. She was training her son to be the next king.

Some explain Proverbs 31 as not being about a woman at all but about wisdom in general. This interpretation is popular partly because Proverbs 31 can be seen as an overwhelming—even impossible—job description for women. For instance, is Proverbs 31 obligating every woman to

- get up before sunrise,
- prepare breakfast for her entire household,
- run a business and buy property,
- knit and sew, and
- work late?

That is a lot—and there's more where that came from! In response to this, many have come to the conclusion that Proverbs 31 could not possibly be describing an actual woman but must be talking about wisdom in general.

It should be noted that Proverbs 31 is a poem. We have seen poetic and figurative language all throughout our study of Proverbs, and Proverbs 31 is no different: It uses specific language in literary ways to allude to more general truths. When reading Proverbs 31, we should be less concerned with the tasks it describes and more concerned about the character, nature, and virtues it celebrates.

The Bottom Line

A wise person learns from a woman of noble character.

EXPERIENCE

You may have noticed that while Proverbs 31 *describes* a woman, it is not *addressed to* a woman; it is addressed to King Lemuel. A woman who possesses these attributes is to be honored and cherished. In many Jewish homes, husbands read Proverbs 31 to their wives or daughters at the end of the week as a way of thanking God for the godly women in their lives. In doing so, a man makes sure to celebrate the most important thing about his wife or daughter: her loyalty to God. That is how this chapter ends: with the reminder that while beauty and charm fade away, honoring and serving the Lord is worthy of never-ending praise!

If you are a young woman reading this, try not to be discouraged by the seemingly impossible job description of Proverbs 31. This proverb is saying that your character, integrity, and loyalty to God are what are most important. If you are a young man reading this, take seriously the advice of Lemuel's mother: When looking for a girlfriend (or a wife!), prioritize wisdom, integrity, and character above all else.

Takeaway and Pray

My takeaway from this experience is

My prayer today is a

__ **REQUEST** __ **CONFESSION** __ **PRAISE**

EXPERIENCE SCRIPTURE

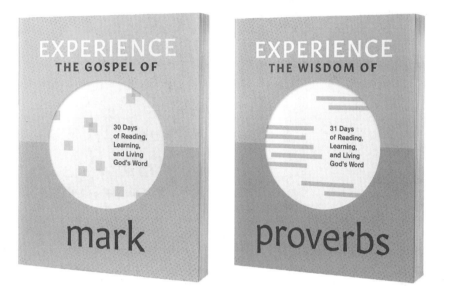

EXPERIENCE
THE GOSPEL OF

30 Days
of Reading,
Learning,
and Living
God's Word

mark

EXPERIENCE
THE WISDOM OF

31 Days
of Reading,
Learning,
and Living
God's Word

proverbs

The Bible is meant to be experienced.
Follow Jesus and the storyline of Scripture
for one month, and see how much your life
will change. Both studies are rooted in
Scripture, accessible, and experiential.

CP1964

THE MESSAGE
STUDENT BIBLE

Understand and enjoy the wisdom and beauty of God's Word! Generation after generation of Bible readers have discovered that the Bible is written not only about us but also to us. In these pages we become insiders in a conversation in which God forms, guides, and ultimately saves us.

THE MESSAGE
FOR GRADUATES

Encounter biblical direction and encouragement for graduates. There are transition points in every life. Graduation is such a transition point: It marks the end of one life stage and the beginning of another. The demands on your life, the complexity of your challenges, the things that bring you joy, and the things that cause you stress—they're different once you've moved from student life to this new season. This book helps you through that transition.

Find these and other great Bibles and Bible resources at messagebible.com.

CP1965